M000310813

GATEWAY
TO THE
MODERN CRONE

JUDE DOWNES

Dedicated to Maggie… the epitome of the Crone…
A woman who taught me how to live life with grace…
humour and wisdom… even when chaos chose
to walk beside her.

First published 2019

Text copyright © Jude Downes 2019
The moral right of the author has been asserted

All rights reserved. No part of this publication may be
reproduced, stored in a retrieval system, or transmitted in any
form or by any means, electronic, mechanical, photocopying,
recording or otherwise, without the prior written permission
of the publisher and copyright holder.

A self published title designed and produced
by Adala Publishing
www.adalapublishing.com.au

ISBN 978-0-6485272-0-6 (Print)
ISBN 978-0-6485272-1-3 (eBook)
ISBN 978-0-6485272-2-0 (PDF)

www.judedownes.com

Crone definition ~ Cambridge dictionary
noun – an unpleasant or ugly old woman.
In stories, an old woman with magic powers.
Other: hag, witch, withered.

Crone in reality
Healer, seer, wise woman, story-weaver,
creator, keeper of mysteries, leader, spiritual
mid-wife, Goddess.

Contents

Part Three – All Crones are Created Different

Part Four – Ceremonies

I TRUDGE SLOWLY THROUGH the forest, feeling old and afraid. I am tired of life. I am discarded, thought of as irrelevant in a world supplicant to youth and beauty. The world embraces the young and shuns the old. I am not really old, but this is how the world sees me, and others like me. I have lived a lifetime of stories, ancient scars that have healed but are seen as scars nonetheless. Some are hidden and others are still a little raw. The young want to deny the scars of the aging, not yet ready to listen to the wisdom held deep within those scars, those stories.

Tears form tracks down my lined face. Perhaps I feel sorry for myself. When did life abandon me? When did I stoop my shoulders and look only to the ground instead of the stars?

The forest is dark and appears damp and lifeless, a reflection of me. Perhaps I am ready to die. Perhaps I am ready to surrender to whatever fate has in store for me.

I seem to be walking a well-worn path but unsure of my destination. The need to be alone with my own thoughts and feelings has been intense these past days. I feel alone with these feelings and yet I am obliquely aware that others also feel this isolating time in life.

I am surrounded in my daily life by family and friends and yet I have never felt so alone. My body is sagging, the lines on my face deepening with every passing year. Changes in my body have hardened and shrivelled my womb. I feel it. I am barren to not only this life-giving force of creation, but my creative spirit seems to have died along with this vital part of being a woman.

I feel at my lowest point. Uninspired, ignored, disrespected by others, invisible, old and ugly, the very epitome of the hag or witch everyone seems to think women of a certain age become.

The path stops abruptly and a huge tree blocks my way forward. As I am gazing down at the ground I begin with the roots and move my eyes slowly skyward… up, up, up and up to the top of the tree before me. It is certainly the biggest tree I have ever seen. I just don't have the energy to journey around her, so I sit with my back against the tree to rest and contemplate my next move. I guess I will have to make my way back to the ordinary world and just be invisible and grow old in an invisible way.

Closing my eyes, I rest awhile. I can't face going back to a world of insignificance just yet. My senses open and I begin to smell the earthy aromas around me. I feel the damp warmth of the forest and the solid trunk of my new tree friend at my back. I am sitting under the canopy of this giant tree and I feel safe somehow.

In what only seems to be minutes to me, my breathing begins to slow and peace threatens to overwhelm me and push away the anxiety and pain that has been building for some time. I sink further and further into that state of peace and now bliss is an underlying force from nature. I am at one with my nature spot. This is the best I have felt in days, or weeks perhaps. I breathe deeply of this new peaceful blissful feeling. I allow it to fill me to overflowing.

After what seems to be only a few moments of sinking into the peace and bliss of this magical place, I think to myself, 'It's time to return back to that other world. I can't sit here all day and wallow in self-pity. I must return and face the world I ran away from an hour or two ago. It must be lunchtime by now'.

They won't have missed me yet, that family of mine. The world is a busy place and I am just a burden to those around me. I must try and take this feeling of deep peace I now feel into that other world. Perhaps this place will become my sanctuary from the overwhelming feelings of being lost and alone in a youth driven world.

Opening my eyes, I am surprised to see it is dusk. Night is just a short time away. The forest is darker than when I arrived and there are eyes peering at me from the surrounding bush. There is more sound than I remember as I walked this lonely trail. Animals come up to sniff my foot before running away to view me from a safe distance. Birds are sitting twittering to me from in the canopy of this massive tree. The eyes peering out from the surrounding bushes seem curious but friendly. An owl wings her way silently to a low branch in the tree. I note her presence as she stares intently at me.

There is movement at my back and I jump up to see what it is as I thought I had my back to the solid trunk of the tree. I hear a chuckle and the canopy reaches down to me. Holding my breath, I fear the tree is about to fall on top of me. A deep comforting woman's voice is coming from the tree but how is that possible? Trees don't talk? And how did it get to be almost nightfall when I only closed my eyes for a few moments? I must be dreaming, I think.

That chuckle again. 'No, you are not dreaming,' the rich voice intones. I jump, startled that this tree knew what I was thinking, let alone that it was speaking.

'You came here, deep in the forest with sadness and pain in your heart. You once felt a vibrant woman and now you feel unloved and unlovable. You feel ignored and intimidated by the very presence of youthful vigour and adoration.'

'Yes,' I stammer. 'That is exactly how I feel. Overlooked, ridiculed, invisible, unfeminine. You name it, I feel it all. I am being pushed aside and I wonder why I am still here if I am not useful.'

My new tree friend bends a little lower and says, 'You are not the first woman to find your way into this forest. You are not the first woman to feel these things. You have entered the forest of the elder, a place of magic and acceptance. A place where you discover the answers to your questions, where healing is as natural as... well... talking with a tree.'

'I am getting old,' I say as I drop my head onto my chest 'and no-one needs or wants me anymore. No-one seeks my advice or sits with me over a cup of tea so I can listen to their stories. No-one wants to listen to my stories even though, through a lifetime of experiences, I have been where they are now.'

'Were you not young once,' the tree asks? 'Yes,' I reply. 'Did you not ignore the elders around you, thinking them unworthy of any attention?' I think back to my youth and mothering days and agree yes, I did indeed think that. With a quick intake of breath, I say, 'oh, I treated elders exactly the same as the young treat me now. So, this is what comes around, goes around. Is that it? You are teaching me that I deserve this, that all older people deserve this because that is the way of life?'

That chuckle again. 'No, this lesson is about you and others like you breaking the cycle of disrespect and invisibility. This is about you and others like you feeling worthy within yourselves and taking charge of your own lives. This is about honouring yourselves as important members of your society and changing the thoughts and feelings of those who will come after you. This is about recognising the Crone within you, the Wise Woman who has a lot to offer her world. This is about standing tall and working with your creative spirit to carve out your next cycle of life, the way you want it to look for you and set about making a difference in your world.

What other people think of you is none of your business. What you think of you is what is important.'

The tree falls silent as I stand there facing it and mulling over her wise words. 'You are right,' I yell. 'I have been wallowing in my own self-pity that I am disregarded in my elder years. I forgot to take charge of my own direction.'

Throwing my head back and raising my arms skyward, I dance a little dance and yell out 'I am the Crone and I am enough!' I am the creator of the next phase of my life. I have a choice. I can just grow old and perhaps frail and at some stage in the advancing years, enter the Goddess waiting room for death to come to me without so much as a murmur of resistance, or, I can embrace the Crone that I am and go out into the world and discover other Crones and change people's perception of getting older. I can encourage people to first honour their inner Crone and then encourage the younger generations to become story listeners, to honour the sanctity of the Wise Woman.

The owl had been sitting quietly on the tree branch, watching me through this meeting with my tree friend. Now she looks me in the eye and turns to pull out one of her feathers. She releases the feather which floats down to me. Taking the feather into my hand, I hear in my mind, 'I am your Crone totem now. Honour me as your messenger between the spirit world and the world of the Crone in your everyday world. I am with you now as you navigate this next honourable cycle.'

With all of this inner dialogue complete, I close my eyes and breathe deeply of my surroundings. After a few moments, I realise that I am sitting once more under the tree. I feel warmth in my body and love, for me, in my heart. Yes, others' reactions to my advancing years are none of my business. The only way something in my life will change, is when I embrace my Crone cycle.

I open my eyes, expecting it to be dark by now and a little apprehensive that I will have to find my way home through a dark forest on a dark, moonless night.

Taking a deep breath, I open my eyes and daylight fills my view. The sun is filtering through the canopy of the tree tops above me indicating it is only noon. Have I slept and it is the day after I entered the forest? Have I fallen into a deep meditation perhaps and only moments have passed? Whatever has happened, I feel happy and at peace. I know my direction now as the Crone. I know she is to be welcomed into my life. I know I am to seek other women who need to also be honoured in this way. I reach behind me and feel only the solid trunk of the tree. A dream, I think. Just a beautiful, healing dream.

I look down at my lap. A single feather is sitting in the contour of my lap. An owl feather. A reminder of the journey ahead. Whether the magic I experienced was a dream, a meditation or real, it is all real in my mind and heart. Standing now, feather held firmly in my hand, I offer my love and gratitude to the tree and the owl and the forest.

I walk back along the path through the forest, seeing it with new eyes, feeling a new feeling in my heart. A feeling that is expressed in the immense love I know is to come. I see now that the forest is teeming with life and light. This reflects my own newly explored feelings. I can't wait to go home and explore the joy of being the Crone… I am enough!

Introduction

THE INTRODUCTORY STORY may be the fantasy of storytelling and yet there is an underlying truth to it. As women age, they appear to become invisible in a world that reveres beauty and youth rather than wisdom and grace.

Before we begin diving into the world of the modern Crone, it is important for me to tell you, right here, right now, that *you* are magnificent, just the way you are. This book is designed to encourage women everywhere to embrace their Crone years and not just accept age as a number in the Goddess waiting room of life and death.

We are born into the time when we will do the most good, gain the most out of our experiences, grow into the woman we are destined to become.

The women who are the Crones right now, were born into a time that offered a steep learning curve, so that when they arrived at this most sacred and final cycle on life's journey, they would be ready to create change in a shaky patriarchal world.

In this time, the Crone feels empowered, vibrant, respected and visible within themselves first. It is about changing personal perceptions surrounding the aging process of the Crone. This is the first step towards empowerment.

I see that we walk the trails of the Ancient Ones. We journey the well-worn ancient paths that lead us to live our sacred soul contracts in vibrant ways. Sometimes within our own environment and sometimes on a greater world stage.

In my visions I see the Crone at the centre of everything with concentric circles radiating outward from that central point. I see 'Crones in the making', women in their forties to early fifties, in the first lot of ripples, followed beyond that by younger women. Each circle, each ripple is a sacred part of the whole of the womanhood journey.

It is important to embrace the Crone and not shy away from the duty of care in guiding the Maiden and the Mother Goddesses who are seeking our wisdom and guidance.

Each woman, regardless of their chronological age will be feeling the wisdom of their own spirit of the

Crone waking up, ready to show them where to be and whom to reach out to and who will show them the way. As the Maiden and the Mother come into their power, they will need the gentle and powerful hand of the Crone at their back, gently guiding the way, gently encouraging them to be the leaders in this world. No-one has to go it alone anymore. Only pride will keep some from seeking the wisdom of those who are the keepers of wisdom.

I see that encouraging existing Crones to remember their journey and empower themselves, in this modern world, is the first vital step on this journey towards self-acceptance and changing the world order to one of peace. It does take time, however every step we take, is a step in the right direction for this to be achieved and become our reality. When those walking the same ancient trails behind the Crone see this self-empowerment and that we truly are transforming the vibrancy of the planet in sound and wise ways, they will bask in the wisdom of the Crone to be empowered in their own lives and create powerful ripples within their own environment.

When a Crone stands in her stillness, the chaos raging around her no longer affects her as much as when she too allowed herself to be caught up in the external chaos of life.

Walking the ancient paths is about remembering the journey and the purpose of the Crone. Those watching and working from within the ripple of sacred wisdom surrounding the Crone, invite a profound life-transforming effect to embrace all who seek her wisdom.

This Gateway to the Modern Crone is one avenue to explore as you embrace the Crone within. This is a book dedicated to the magic of life through ritual, symbols, story-weaving, invoking the Goddess and the Crone and ceremony for Crones and Crones in the making.

My aim in writing this book is to encourage women to remember not only that they are Goddess, embracing peace and power within but that they are moving into a powerful time in their life journey, their Crone years.

This guide for the modern Crone is not a history book of the Matriarch, the hag, the witch and the Crone, rather it offers intuitive guidance, with the encouragement of the Crone and the Ancient Ones on embracing the magnificent Crone that you are in this modern world. It is aimed at the modern Crone navigating a world that long ago lost the ability to offer respect and recognise the value they bring to this world as the wisdom keepers, the story-weavers and the healers.

It all begins with self-respect and self-recognition as women who are truly worthy of carrying the mantle of Crone. When self-acceptance kicks in, then we can begin to change the status quo of the world. We can begin to shine that Crone light outward to change a jaded patriarchal-ruled world.

I know many men who honour the Goddess and honour the women in their lives as the embodiment of the Archetypal Goddess, Wise Woman, Crone. When we accept self, we teach our partners, our children and our grandchildren that women and men, when they embrace the gentle and yet powerful Crone aspect of life, that life will indeed get a whole lot better.

The key is to discover the balance of the feminine and the masculine rather than seeing one as more important than the other. Otherwise we could be in danger of swapping a patriarchal rule for a matriarchal rule instead of seeking equality, balance. We need both.

You *are* magnificent... just as you are.

I see the earth as both the Mother Goddess and the Crone Mother. The Crone Mother first came to me at age fifty-one when I was running a women's retreat. Prior to participants arriving, I climbed one of the steep hills at the back of the magnificent property. As

I reached the top, an older woman appeared to me and told me she was the Crone Mother.

She represented herself to me as an older woman in a cloak, with a hawk and a staff. Perhaps showing herself to me in an atypical manner for that time. As she walked with me, she had one succinct message for me that I remember. A message to trust.

Exactly one week after this fabulous event, my father died suddenly and unexpectedly. Trust indeed. It was nine years, in the year I turned sixty, before she returned to again ask me to trust. Now the time was right for me to embrace my own Crone and to work with women who have entered into their Crone years. Crone Mother, as she calls herself, is now always with me, pushing me to write, coming to me as the owl, guiding me to create and facilitate Crone Gatherings and Ceremonies, a Rite of Passage.

Now is the time to rise and show that the Crone is worthy of deep respect, of being visible.

Prologue

$\mathcal{E}$ACH OF THE four sacred working parts in this book work with the Crone through Story-weaving, the Modern Crone, the five aspects of life and working with ceremony.

It is my aim to make the Crone real, visible and respected as she once more accepts the mantle of Wise Woman, Healer, Seer, Spiritual Midwife, Story-weaver and more.

In Gateway to the Modern Crone I work with practical Crone magic through meditation, messages from the Crone, invocation, ritual and ceremony and connecting with the earth.

The word Crone means Crown and it is thought that this crowning represented being Queen and also wisdom emanating through the 'crown' of the head. She has so often, throughout history, been called a hag and a witch and it seems that these terms are interchangeable and denigrated in today's world.

In this modern world, we can still blame a patriarchy for creating a society where the Crone is declared invisible and irrelevant in a world where beauty and youth are revered, however I can see that, generally speaking, women have accepted that this is the status quo and whilst they don't like being relegated to just being considered old, they so often do nothing to awaken their inherent nature of the sassy, sensual, sexy, vibrant older woman who has so much to offer this world. What we can do, is rise above the patriarchy and societal views of who is valued and embrace our own power as an effective and esteemed member of today's modern society.

I often ask older women how they feel about the word Crone, and it immediately makes them shudder as they associate it with the hag, the old woman, the witch. I then ask them how they feel about the words Wise Woman and they feel very comfortable being called a Wise Woman. I *love* the word Crone because to me, it represents the wise woman and it also holds power as someone to be revered for her story-weaving, her healing ways, her wise advice, her knowing and poise and grace.

We only dishonour the aging Crone because we have been taught and shown throughout our lifetime and through the memories of our Ancestral ties that the Wise Women of society are irrelevant.

Being aged doesn't necessarily suddenly make older people nicer, wiser, accepting of others or change their worldly outlook. Being a Crone is something that emerges from deep within the core of each woman, where acceptance of self first is honoured and remembered as worthy, and where she is ready to take on the mantle of Crone and see herself as beautiful, sensual, sassy and worthy as she embraces an exciting time in her life. New goals and dreams are a part of her Crone life.

My aim is to encourage older women to embrace this time through rites of passage and practical Crone workings. This book is available for *all* women, whether they are in their Crone time or Crones in the making years or younger women recognising the power of the Crone and accessing the Crone spirit present in their life. Many of the magical workings in this book can be adapted to all ages of womanhood.

I do not follow a particular spiritual path or label myself in any direct way. Rather, I see myself as a child, a woman of the earth and my connection with her representation as Earth Goddess and Crone Mother is a strong bond. This Gateway to the Modern Crone book, is my way of creating what I know to be right for me.

May you also discover that connection that will bring about peace on earth through your association with the spirit of the Crone.

Enjoy the Crone journey. It's a powerful one! I honour the Crone in me and I honour her in you.

Jude

Jude

$\mathcal{I}$ AM AN ORDINARY woman, who lives in a little cottage on a mountain surrounded by mountains with the love of my life, my dog Moo and cat Mao with daily visits from wombats, kangaroos, deer and eagles. I also happen to connect with the Earth Mother, the Goddess and the Crone and have extraordinary experiences mixed in with my everyday world. I am very blessed in my Crone years.

I believe in the magic of life and I believe in our ability to create something sacred from the ashes of our life lessons and challenges. I believe we can live an extraordinary life within an ordinary world. It is all about perception.

I am a woman who built a labyrinth and a stone circle on our property for magical women's workings. A woman who invites women here for ritual and ceremony that I have written, workshops I have created from my own creative spirit.

I am a woman who has made mistakes over my many years on this earth and I am a woman who has picked myself up each time I fell over and got on with life, to the best of my ability.

I am an ordinary woman whose only claim to being anything is as someone who loves sitting with the Earth Mother and connecting with her, listening to her with my heart. Something I have consciously done for over twenty years.

I am a woman whose passion lies in the empowerment of women in a mundane world; in the raising of awareness that you/me/we are vibrant, sensual, sassy women who can make a difference in our own world, which ultimately ripples out into the greater world. I believe this with all of my heart.

I am an ordinary woman who feels the rise of the Sacred Feminine, who feels the visibility rising for the archetypal spirit of the Crone. By honouring the ordinary and real in my own journey, I honour the fabulous everyday women who are ready to embrace their vibrant sassy nature. Rather than being alone in the mundane, wondering if this is all life has to offer the aging woman, they become a part of the collective of women embracing their Divinely Feminine self. Now, that's extraordinary.

I once asked an Aboriginal Elder I was staying with why I love sitting and connecting with the earth so much. She replied that it was because I was a white woman with a black heart. It took me many years before I fully understood and embraced this. It is only now, in my Crone years that I get it, and this is my own take on what that means, not only for me, but for the many women who are drawn to connect with Mother Earth in however that looks for them.

When the world is run by an out-of-control patriarchy, it is necessary to work from inside the system (being born into that same culture) to affect lasting change. This is why we are living in the times we are. We came here to create this change, or at least the beginnings of it within the bodies and hearts of who we are. Whatever the beautiful colour of our skin, whatever our chronological age, we live in these amazing times of transformation and our hearts are all the same, singing to the earth with the same voice and a strong desire for peace on earth.

As women, we are growing into our voices. As Crones we are ready to be vital, vibrant, wisdom keepers that can and will assist the transition of the planet to a place of peace. It takes time but it is about the remembering who we are.

I am an ordinary woman, who seems to know 'stuff', because that is what I came here to do, to achieve. My role is one of helping women empower themselves and the way I do that, is by being a 'Healer with Words'.

It is quite a journey we are all navigating so let's do it together and help each other up. It's the only way!

How to Work with
Gateway to the Modern Crone

*T*HERE ARE FOUR sacred working parts in Gateway to the Modern Crone that are designed to take the reader on a journey as she enters her wonderful and sacred Crone years. This book is for women who are entering or well and truly in their Crone years. Women who resonate with the Crone and who are perhaps in their years as the Elder Crone. I see the Crone as a woman in her fifties or sixties who is perhaps still working, still caring for children and grandchildren and yet, she is also now also the keeper of the wise blood. I see the Elder Crone as the woman in her seventies and beyond, who has earned respect as the wise one, the story-weaver. People come to her to listen to her stories.

It is also for women who are in their emerging Crone years or younger women wanting to step into their power so that when they reach their Crone years, they already know their power. Women of all ages who are feeling the pull of the spirit of the Crone. Women who are seeking to empower themselves; their journey.

Part One is Story-weaving. A collection of stories from my own life and a message from the Crone and Journey to the Crone, an opportunity to close your eyes and feel her presence.

Part Two is filled with invocations, incantations, meditations, mini ceremony, a come sit at my table recipe, a list of essential tools for the Crone journey and creation to assist you to move with the spirit of the Crone years through magical workings. Working with energy that will reflect deeply with your everyday life.

Part Three is accessing the five aspects of the Crone as I see them as they connect with the four cardinal directions and the central soul fire that I associate with the stars.

Part Four is the creation of three ceremonies. A Rite of Passage Gathering and Ceremony, a connecting with the Goddess Ceremony and a Healing Trauma Ceremony. The Gateway to the Crone Ceremony is an adapted version of the Gathering and Ceremony I have written and facilitate here in the High Country of Victoria, Australia, for women ready to walk through that fabulous Gateway.

Be in your stillness to walk the sacred and ancient paths of the Ancestors, the Ancient Ones. Be aware of your own spirit of the Crone. Honour the Goddess, Mother Earth and the Crone. They will guide you well along your Crone path.

PART ONE

Story-weaving

Stories, Messages from the Crone, Journey with the Crone

*I*MAGINE… YOU ARE seated with five other women around the kitchen table. The table is set. The teapot is on the table. Six beautiful teacups and saucers are set, all shining and pretty on a lovely brightly coloured tablecloth. Napkins, perfectly folded, lie to the side of the tea plate.

The hostess pours the tea as a guest begins to explore the delicacies artfully arranged on the many gorgeous plates. Plates that are placed strategically around the centre of the well laid table so that every woman present can have her fill without reaching down the length of the table for a morsel of delectable home baked treats.

The hostess begins to chat, another joins in and yet another, between sips of hot delicious tea, leans forward in anticipation of the story emerging. There is so much to share. Laughter begins to bubble unharnessed.

Bawdy comments intersperse a sad tale, bringing more laughter. A tear drops. Silence, compassion and sound advice are the gifts of the moment as those present offer support. Unconditional support.

All present know that what is shared at the table, stays at the table. It is the secret unspoken code of gatherings such as these.

You could be forgiven for thinking that I have described a table for ladies from our grandmother's day and yet, it is happening right now, these gatherings of the Wise Woman, the Crone.

When women gather together in such a ritualistic way, serving tea (or coffee) and a plate of deliciousness to share, they are setting a clear intention that a special calling to order of the Crones, the Grandmothers, the Wise Ones is about to proceed. The only rules are to have fun, laugh as much as possible, share stories, cry, tell bawdy jokes, solve the problems of the world, be a keeper of secrets and be as outrageous as possible.

There is safety in this Crone gathering. The Crone-hood, this sisterhood of Wise Ones will bring joy, love, laughter, tears, hugs, compassion and in all of this beauty of connecting the Crones, lies an inherent quality that is the story-weaver.

THIS SHARING OF stories is an important part of a woman's ritual gathering. To have lived a lifetime of experiences sees you as a key player in the story-weaving journey. You are a storyteller.

The second part to story-weaving is being a good story listener. This second part is often the hardest. So often I see women sharing an important story, an important part of themselves, wanting to be truly heard and yet someone present is not really listening. All they want to do is jump in and share a similar story of their own.

It is a gift to be a good story listener. Being a story listener honours the story teller as worthy. She acknowledges that she has heard and understood the story teller without interruption, judgement or advice that has not necessarily been sought.

The following stories are true and most of them are *my* stories. Stories that illustrate times in my life and how I navigated life's journey. Each story is followed by a message from the Crone and Journey with the Crone. Read the message and the journey, close your eyes and feel her presence.

I hope you enjoy the Crone journey through Gateway to the Modern Crone.

I Had a Dream

*M*ANY YEARS AGO, when I was in my forties, I had a dream that was so profound that I never forgot it. It was one of those dreams where you wake up with the vibrant detail etched in your mind and heart.

The dream began with the younger me, as I was then, sitting in the passenger seat of a car driven by my Crone self. We were sitting in four lanes of traffic, and it wasn't going anywhere. The traffic had come to a standstill. Everyone was just following the crowd, as they do, and waiting to inch along as they thought they were heading towards their destination and it would take a while. Everyone was heading in much the same direction. The elder version of me decided she'd had enough of following the crowd and pulled out to the other side of the road into oncoming traffic. It was pretty light traffic coming the other way and even though the younger me was frightened, the older me just floored it and raced to the head of the traffic. We arrived at a very special place where only a handful of people had arrived. An angel handed me a blanket and said rest now as it is going to be a while before others arrive.

I have never forgotten that dream because now I *am* the older me, in my Crone years and it has become clear over the past few years about what I am supposed to be doing and that is working with women to remember their inner own Goddess and embrace the spirit of the Crone.

The Goddess, the Earth Mother and the Crone had a big plan for me, but I needed to sort 'stuff' out first. I have discovered over many years that the Goddess, our guides, Angels, the Ancestors, the Ancient Ones or whoever we associate with, show us our potential future. When we accept and honour it, the vision or feeling, they rub their metaphorical hands together and say, right, now let's get on with clearing some attachment to the old stories. Let's show her just how the lessons learned over a lifetime have seeded her potential over these many years and now she is ready to honour her sacred soul contract and do what, at a deep soul level, she knows she came here to do. We need to heal the way forward. This is when we dive deep and grow into who we are destined to be, with the guidance of the Goddess, the Earth Mother, the Crone and all of our guidance.

MESSAGES FROM THE CRONE

The dreamer in you is sending you on symbolic pathways to assist you in discovering your new direction in life. This is the powerful way to dream the beautiful dreams of the Crone journey.

JOURNEY WITH THE CRONE

I am silent. A dream held within a dream. What is real, what is not? The symbols I see are real, the feelings I feel are real. All are showing me my Crone direction. My sacred soul contract is laid out before me. The symbols are the language of the spirit realms. They speak directly to my soul. I breathe deeply and the scene changes, it is more vibrant somehow, showing me what needs to be done, the steps I need to take. My daydreams, my night-time dreams show me the way. My contract is set, my purpose is now being fulfilled. I understand.

I am the Crone. I honour my sacred place in this time of life. I am at peace.

Fifty Changes Everything

*E*VERYONE IN LIFE comes with a back-story. Those stories that helped shape us and our journey. The good stories, the not so good stories and the downright out and out ugly stories. We all have 'em! They keep us real.

This story is one of those back stories that shifted me into my Crone years with a slightly savage push I thought. I was stubborn and proud and didn't want to 'fail' at yet another relationship. I didn't want to see it for what it truly was, another learning curve on the hard road of life and yet my guidance needed me to shrug off the old and outworn and instead I stubbornly added a bandaid! Sigh.

Fifty was supposed to be one of those times of happy transition from my forties into a new decade, into the time where I would begin my journey into embracing the early journey into the Crone, to step onto a path that would lead me into menopause and all of the changes that would come with a new life cycle. A secret revealed at that time turned my world upside down.

However, instead of stepping away from the energy of exposed secrets and a relationship that was destructive, I sought to repair it. It would take another six years before the break was finally made, by him, and I was set free to be the person I always was underneath but had buried under increasing weight problems and insecurities.

The signposts were all there around my fiftieth birthday that I should begin this new cycle free and clear of this destructive relationship, but I buried my metaphorical head in the sand and set about 'fixing' the relationship, which in reality was only a bandaid.

Dragonfly is a big totem, a fabulous messenger for me and he heralded the onset to this betrayal when he flew into my office at the end of the day, one warm summer evening. A large bright blue dragonfly. I searched everywhere for him but could not find him. I knew that his sudden appearance meant that something major was about to happen in my life. Dragonfly medicine is about seeing beyond the illusions that colour our life, seeing the reality of situations and the colour blue is, to me, about speaking truth. A deep breath and I headed home, wondering what was coming my way, never really expecting dragonfly's message to be of the nature that did indeed come my way.

Within days of dragonfly's appearance, I discovered that the fear of loss that I had long held in this relationship had their roots in secrets, betrayal, pain and hurt. Years before, I too had caused pain, so the irony was not lost on me but right now, a spiritual understanding was not my closest friend.

Over the next couple of months, every time I thought we had healed the problem and perhaps could get back on track in our relationship, dragonfly would come knocking on my door, literally, to say, you are not through this yet. One would come and tap on the lounge window just as a reminder of the healing I personally needed to do and that all was not right in my world. When I got into my car to back out of my driveway, one would hover over the windscreen of my car for a minute or two. They seemed to be 'in-my-face' all the time, wherever I went, as if to say, we are not done with you yet.

Just before my fiftieth birthday, I decided to go horse riding for the first time in many years. There was just me and two lovely young ladies who escorted me on the trail ride. It was supposed to be a celebration, just for me. At one point, we cantered through a creek and hundreds of dragonflies took off from the water and surrounded me. We weren't done yet it seemed, and I felt sick to my stomach. More betrayal came out and as always, I thought I was the one who had to fix it because he buried his head in the proverbial sand.

Three months after we first dove down into the depths of hell, I went for a walk to my favourite place, on a rock in the middle of a creek near home.

As I walked the one km to my destination, dragon-fly flew by my side. As I turned off the path towards the creek, another dragonfly guided my way. I stood on my rock and a large yellow and black dragonfly came to me, flew around me and left. I sang an Aboriginal song I knew about earth connection. This dragonfly came again and flew around me and with my physical eyes, I saw this dragonfly split into two separate dragonflies. They both flew around me and left. One dragonfly came once more, landed at my feet for a few moments before taking off, flying around me and leaving for the last time. Dragonfly is also known as nature's shapeshifter.

Perhaps I didn't want to see the clear message at that time, that I was supposed to be on my own. The singular dragonfly split into two and one left. It is clear now, in hindsight of course, but at the time I just wanted to fix things, to mend something broken. It must be my fault, right? I put a bandaid over the whole relationship and set about trying to be bigger than that, to heal everything, for both of us.

In the months before he finally left, six years later, my partner came home with a large blue dragonfly. It had flown in the car window and sat on his steering wheel the whole forty km drive home. He placed it on his hand when he arrived home and it immediately flew to my throat and sat there like a large pendant. Blue for truth. Throat, needing to speak the truth. This was an uh-oh kind of thing. Another big blue dragonfly telling me about change, about illusion, about truth.

Less than a year later, at the ripe old age of fifty-six, the bandaid was well and truly ripped off and it hurt. I grieved the loss of this relationship, even though in my heart and soul I knew our soul contract was up. So, I set about healing myself and learning to be on my own. I knew in my heart that I would eventually welcome one more relationship into my life but first I had things to do and experience as a middle aged, single, overweight and damaged woman.

Over the ensuing seventeen months, I shed 22 kg, my skin glowed, *I* glowed. I laughed and played. I wrote my From Grief to Goddess book and Healing cards,

I manifested the exact house I wanted to rent at the price I wanted, including the quirkiness I craved, so I could live overlooking the great Southern Ocean. I sat for hour upon hour watching the waves, gentle at times, wild and untamed at others as I healed my inner Goddess. She was battered and bruised by abandonment and betrayal, but I wasn't perfect. I had made some big errors in judgement in my life too. I must have deserved this mistreatment, these lies and deceit. Right? Absolutely not!

It was through my own journaling and the cathartic writing of my book and cards that I began my journey into truly understanding myself . For the first time in my life, I wasn't trying to please someone else. Just me. I only had to concern myself with me. It was all about me, me, me! I had traversed menopause with relative ease, I'd had the most extraordinary experiences in the desert ceremonies in Central Australia, the energy of which helped me through it with ease and I connected deeply with the earth.

I worked with ceremony and workshops and yet, through all of that I wasn't fully aware of my inner Goddess in any real way *or* that I was at the beginning of my Crone years and that this separation, this very painful time was like a baptism of fire so to speak as I awakened something primal and ancient and deeply feminine from within the depths of my own soul.

Hindsight is a beautiful gift don't you think? I can see it all clearly now. I had something bigger to achieve in life and the baggage of being immersed in this negative relationship was firmly taken out of my hands. Until he left, I kept fooling myself into believing the bandaid was firmly in place and all was right with the world, my world anyway. My next cycle, the Crone cycle, truly began in that moment of revelation.

Sixty however, was *the* best milestone birthday of my life. The day I turned sixty, I knew my path was set. I felt different. It was a tangible thing, this sixty-gig, and I felt it, loved it and knew something magical had awakened within me.

I smiled all the time. I had married the love of my life just one year after our first meeting, I lived on a mountain top surrounded by mountains and I was working in magical energy to write and create workshops and ceremonies in this enchanting creative environment. Winter snows, autumn gold, summer green, spring colour. I was right at home amongst it all. I had known this time would come a lifetime ago. I just had a few things to deal with along the way to get here. To get 'here', I needed a fairly clear path to travel and that didn't involve old ways of living my life.

We never fully get to our destination as we are always a story in progress and there are many chapter rewrites along the way as we refine the journey and that's great, because the more we learn and accept ourselves as worthy, regardless of our age, the more we are happy with where we are on life's journey. It's about discovering that place of peace and joy within, even when chaos is raging around us. This is where women can offer inspired wisdom and practicalities to others on their journey into becoming the Crone.

I journaled all of my stories and inspirations and dreams and each time I looked back over my journey, I could see a story emerging. Each journal entry was a gift to me, to change direction, to continue a certain direction, to stop and rest, to move forward, to value-add to what I was doing in my life, to warn me in times of trouble (not that I always took notice) and to keep my faith in my journey strong.

Story-weaving will keep the threads of your journey strong so that you weave each thread into a beautiful tapestry representing your life. When you pull all the threads together, you will understand why certain events happen in life and that each thread is an important part of the overall tapestry of life. Journaling the stories will keep them vibrant and clear.

MESSAGES FROM THE CRONE

Aspire to be the best version of you that you can be. Every small victory is a step heralding beautiful change in your life.

JOURNEY WITH THE CRONE

I open my eyes and night is still upon me. I peer into the inky darkness, instantly alert as I begin to recall my dream. Its vivid nature inspires me to switch on my light and write. The Crone came to me in my dream state to offer wisdom for the journey ahead. I have been in turmoil about decisions looming on my near horizon, and as always, her gentle wisdom is shining a light on the right decisions for me to make. Decisions that will offer me the best outcomes for the next steps to take.

Every detail, every colour, every symbol from my dream is important to my journey. I complete my writing; switch off my light and return to sleep. My dream is recorded for me to begin to unravel when first light breaks. I am at peace now with the decisions I will make with the assistance of the wisdom of the Crone.

I am the Crone. I honour my sacred place in this time of life. I am at peace.

The Last Bleed and
Desert Healing

*T*HE DESERT CEREMONIES call me once more. I am to journey to the desert one last time to be in ceremony with the Elders, camping in swags and tents, at a sacred women's place around 250 km from Uluru in Central Australia.

There are less than thirty of us on this final trip. I am fifty-three years old. This year of fifty-three has been challenging with my health, having recently undergone numerous tests for heart problems. At first the doctors tell me there is a problem and then on further testing no, all is well. On the strength of that diagnosis, I book my third trip to the desert.

Heading towards my destination, I am sitting in a plane that is loud and vibrating through my entire body. In my quiet, excited anticipation for the journey ahead, chest pains begin once more. Oh no, not now, please not now. I am heading into the desert where there were no amenities, no doctors, no emergency department. I think to myself, what am I doing? I could give in to the pains and say I can't go, I'm too sick but a decision is made just as swiftly as thought occurs and I don't tell anyone.

Several of the women I am to be travelling with, want to walk the base of Uluru but I am breathless and feeling very unwell. I smile and say I just want to meditate with the rock, and I sit in front of a cave and enjoy my meditation. Please pain, go away. It doesn't.

We journey over thick red dusty roads in Toyota troop carriers. There are eight of us in the back of each of these 4WDs which have two long seats along the insides of the vehicle. We have our swags and tents, a small luggage bag and ten litres of water each piled in with us. It is a tight squeeze. It is an all-day drive ahead of us over this dusty road. I see the reverse angle of Kata Juta as we leave the relative safety of Uluru. I am still having chest pains and I do indeed wonder what I am thinking. However, I still remain silent.

As we near our destination, the trailer we are towing with our supplies throws an axle. After considerable discussion, there is a light meal in the dark before we set up camp for the night and I crawl into my little tent, exhausted and in pain. As I lay there contemplating my predicament, I see the spirit of an Aboriginal woman lean over me and place her hands over me. Instead of feeling fearful, I just smile to myself, roll over and fall into a deep peaceful slumber as though it is the most natural thing on earth.

On waking the next morning, there is no sign of my spirit healer and my chest pains have gone. I didn't have them again for many years. My energy has returned and I can immerse myself fully in the experience of being in the desert ceremonies.

This desert morning looks more vibrant and awash with colour than anything I have experienced in quite some time. The red of the earth and the blue of the sky are intense and beautiful to me.

Abandoning our broken trailer, we load up the 4WDs with the rest of our supplies; our food and extra water for the five days ahead. We don't have far to travel to our destination. Setting up camp again is easy. The power of the land beneath us is palpable.

The women are gracious in sharing their land and their ceremonies with us.

My period arrives on the day we are to begin ceremony. Menopause began eighteen months ago and my periods have been irregular so I really didn't know it was going to arrive at this time.

If we are bleeding, we are not permitted to participate in ceremony and we become the observer of these sacred rites. It is a powerful time for a woman to bleed. I am happy enough with this as this was a big trip to this very sacred land and all I have endured to get here. As a part of our journeying together we are taken to sacred sites that emit immense power and this is enough for me.

Five days of beautiful connection with the Elders, the earth and ceremony and we return to Uluru. This time I am ready to walk the base of her and I do so with ease. I am healed and unbeknownst to me at that time, I have also completed my final period. This very sacred place was a place of healing and emergence for me. What more profound way could there be to finish my menses than in a sacred women's place in the desert witnessing the desert ceremonies. All women need to honour their final menses in a sacred way that feels right for them.

A woman's capability to create does not shrivel up with the loss of her menses, rather it just changes its flow from blood flow to holding the wise blood. It is now held within and is available to be channelled into creative energy. A very sacred and powerful time in a woman's life, particularly when it is honoured in a sacred way. This is a powerful understanding of the beginnings of becoming a Crone.

MESSAGES FROM THE CRONE

Your wise and creative spirit is still held close to you in your womb, whether you still have a physical womb or not. It is spiritual and powerful as you hold your blood close to you now. Awaken the beauty of your creative spirit and let it flow out into your greater world. You *are* the Wise Blood.

JOURNEY WITH THE CRONE

The desert calls to me. I feel her sacred presence inviting me to be close to her. I sit on the warm earth, closing my eyes. I breathe deeply of the scented warm desert air. My breath slows and I feel my connection to this sacred space. The power of the earth rises to greet me, filling my body with power and the essence of the Goddess and the Crone.

I metaphorically release my last blood flow into the earth. A gift to honour my journey that is now as the Wise Blood, the keeper of the wisdom of the Crone.

I am the Crone. I honour my sacred place in this time of life. I am at peace.

Love of my Life

MY MANUSCRIPT FOR From Grief to Goddess is complete and at my publishers. It's time to make a decision. Stay in the tiny coastal town where I am living and that has been home for the past seventeen months or move back to the city.

I am fifty-seven years old, I don't have a regular 'job' and my money is limited. Do I play it safe and stay here and perhaps study something to get me into a new career or should I get a job or perhaps trust my intuition and move? Decisions need to be made about the next phase of my life.

I decide and I pack up my life, again. My belongings are stored for now, until I find my 'home'. Goodbye beautiful coast. I will miss you. You have been both a catalyst for intense change and a nurturing gift of healing a part of my life that is no longer required. I know it is time to begin a new life.

The truck has left with my possessions and I stand and watch it journey down the road and out of sight. My car is packed to overflowing and I squeeze my gorgeous red furry angel Moo into a space in the back seat. I smile broadly as we begin our three-and-a half-hour drive back to the city. I know in my heart and soul that we are driving towards our destiny, I just don't know what that might look like in reality yet. We are off on our next adventure.

I meet the love of my life within a few short weeks of moving. Two weeks later we are sharing his home and slowly it becomes my home too. We marry one year later on our property in front of forty guests. Sometimes, when your intuition says jump in, you just do it and then figure it all out later.

The journey to get to this point was never going to be an easy one. It never is. You think to yourself, so this time, I will fall madly in love and live happily ever after but in real life, there are always obstacles to clear first.

In the safety on my isolated coastal home and the loneliness I felt, I had an inner knowing that I had one more partner to come in this lifetime. In the months prior to my previous partner leaving, I had danced along the shoreline on a lonely beach as Whitney Houston's 'I Wanna Dance with Somebody (who loves me)' played in my head. It was one of the times where something bubbles up inside you and you can't help but be pushed to just, well, dance and sing out loud on a lonely beach. It was a little confusing as I was still partnered at the time, but I knew it wasn't about him. He just didn't dance. Confusing? Yes.

In my post-separation loneliness, I wrote a list of qualities I wanted in a life partner. I was very specific. I wanted honesty, deep love, loyalty, good-looking and tall would be a bonus and oh yes, I asked that he would challenge me in the best possible way and call me on any BS rather than agree with everything I uttered or did in my life. This would be a nice change I think to myself. Someone who makes me think about things and who supports me in my life choices.

Cranking up my favourite music I danced around my loungeroom, overlooking the great Southern Ocean, with its majesty and ever-changing, at times calm and at other times intense beauty, and I would see this man in my mind's eye. We always danced together in my heart and soul.

We met online and clicked from the moment we talked on the phone. In a phone call he told me that he couldn't wait to meet me and he would be there with bells on. When he arrived to pick me, he actually had bells tied to his boots so they tinkled when he walked. Cute.

I had kissed some frogs, as the saying goes, in the preceding months before meeting him, so I was a little shy of being hurt. My old wounds surfaced and I resisted his charm. So, when he leaned across the table to me and said, 'I think this is going well don't you?' I took a deep breath and said, 'I don't think there is any chemistry.' His crestfallen face was very confused as our talks on the phone had gone so well. To his credit, we still continued our date day and of course the more I got to know him over the course of the day, the more I liked what I saw and he also gave the best hugs. I opened my heart and jumped right in, boots and all.

I knew from the beginning he was an Asperger and I was brave. I researched it, read some books and promptly threw them all away. I knew I could handle anything, right? There was such a beautiful connection between us that we could get through anything, right? In the first few months, we would really push each other's buttons and I was confused. He would push me and push me and I didn't understand enough about Asperger's to know when he was in 'overload' where his mind could not cope with too much overstimulation. I didn't know, at that time, that the more I asked questions or pushed back, the deeper the overload from mind turmoil would become, and we would have a big argument. One day he pushed too far and I threw a pepper shaker at the wall near him and peppercorns flew all over the room. Peppercorns were still being discovered months later, which became quite funny. We called it the 'Peppercorn Incident'. However, it was at that breaking point that a corner was turned.

We retreated to our corners to lick our emotional wounds and came out hugging with new understanding. We loved each other and somehow, I began to understand the mind of my Aspie. From that breaking moment, we changed and my calm and my intuitive understanding, rather than an understanding from any book, helped our relationship. He began to calm as he realised what deep love meant, which is not easy for an Aspie to understand.

I learned to recognise the different Aspie aspects and behaviours and most of the time, I understood what I needed to do or say (or not do and say at a given time), to help in times of Asperger stress. Life became mostly calm with truth and trust and unconditional love as solid foundations. Something I personally desperately needed.

He also ticked every single box on my life partner list, including challenging me. He called me on my stuff, just as much as I called him on his. Some of the things I thought were true for me could be thought about and taken under advisement. He helped me look at the bigger picture of my life. He challenged me to be the very best version of me. He challenged me to keep going. He believed in me and supported me in every way, and I loved him for it. He told me I didn't know what I was capable of, yet. His intuition was something I craved as my equal and I respected his messages even if I didn't always agree.

I would say, 'but I *am* happy.' He would say, 'yes, but there is so much more to you that you are not yet aware of.' I couldn't see it at the time or understand it because if you don't have a measure for something, how can you possibly know what that something is. I have grown immeasurably because someone, my life partner believed in me. He could truly 'see' me, even if he couldn't explain it to me. He still does.

One year after we met, we married on our property, outside under the tall gums with the mountains beyond. The night before our wedding there was a huge thunderstorm.

'Do you have a plan B if it rains?' people asked in the months leading up to the wedding. 'It will be fine,' I would reply.

Thunder, lightning and rain rolls away to reveal a vibrant rainbow in the valley below us. The day of our wedding dawns bright and sunny. Perfect.

A beautiful ceremony seals our love, including a hand fasting, dancing in the paddock, a pink cake and lots of love and laughter. All with ease and grace. When everything falls into place effortlessly like all our wedding plans did, right down to the weather, you know it is right.

Life on occasion has its challenges. Every relationship does but this marriage of twin souls is full of deep love and support and tenderness and romance. When you get what you ask for, you work with it rather than against it because it truly is a gift from the Divine. Why ditch the gift when it arrives in a different package to how you thought it would arrive, when it always has the potential to grow into something truly beautiful!

MESSAGES FROM THE CRONE

A gift of love doesn't always arrive neatly packaged. Sometimes you need to take off the outer wrapping to see the beautiful gift shining inside. A gift that keeps on giving of itself is a truly wonderful gift indeed. Sometimes you need to see your own gift reflected in the eyes of another.

JOURNEY WITH THE CRONE

The music plays softly in the background. I am drawn to dance, to throw back my head and give myself to the music. The earth beneath me is pulsating with vibrant energy. I love the woman, the Crone that I am.

I am the Crone. I honour my sacred place in this time of life. I am at peace.

Sacred Arrivals, Departures and a Sacred Crowning

STEPPING INTO MY Crone years has come with many changes, including a sacred birth and a death, opposite ends of life's fabulous spectrum. It has also brought the gift of honouring a beautiful Crone in her final months with a sacred crowning.

These are three stories I will share with you. They are stories about times in my Crone years where I was placed in unusual situations in order to get me to do what the spirit realms were asking of me. I was told ahead of time that these situations were where I needed to be and I didn't push them and yet, as you will see in the stories below, that knowledge and how they unfolded was not by my design. I know that these sacred journeys were a part of my soul contract and a part of what would be my 'work' when I stepped up to the plate so to speak, the year I turned sixty!

A SACRED BIRTH

I step back. I know I am supposed to be at the birth of my second granddaughter, but I step back, staying quiet, not knowing how to approach this most sacred of journeys with her parents to be.

If I am supposed to be there, I will be. That is my thought. Not to aggressively push myself forward. This is not my way. The date is close and I have surrendered all thoughts of being there.

My working life is in an environment where taking time off is often met with a frown and disapproval. Anxiety keeps me compliant with the wishes of the company.

In recent months I have been experiencing heart pain and on consultation, a decision was made that I had something wrong with my heart wall and an angiogram was ordered.

It is a rare day I take away from my job to attend a cardiology appointment. Sitting quietly in the waiting room waiting for my appointment, my phone rings.

'We are in labour,' my son says, 'on our way to hospital now.'

'I'm not at work today.' I tell him.

'Drop by the hospital when you are done with your appointment,' he invites. I don't need to be asked twice. I'm there.

I sit with them as labour develops. Standing to leave to let them have their privacy they both say 'Stay. We would love you to be here for her birth.' Once more, I don't need to be invited twice. I sit on the periphery, holding sacred space as contractions become more intense. It's time to push and I keep holding that sacred space as my beautiful tiny granddaughter enters the world.

As she arrives, so do her two totem animals. I see an elephant and a young lion standing within a sacred circle in the birthing room. Interestingly they don't seem to take up a lot of space which makes me giggle. My thoughts drift back to the night when my first granddaughter was born.

My son calls and informs me, 'we are in labour.' My first grandchild, I am excited. I have no idea how long it will be before she is born, so I head to bed.

Movement in my bedroom wakes me suddenly. Standing between my bed and the wall, in a space of around a metre, is a rhinoceros and a huge stag with a large set of antlers. I didn't even think about how they could possibly fit into that tiny space even though I saw them as full size!

I knew in that moment that my granddaughter had been born. Sometime later my son called to tell me she had indeed been born and the time she was born, which of course, was exactly the time I saw her animals appear.

The magic of life's journey is a fabulous and rich journey if you open your heart and mind to the endless possibilities that exist beyond our mortal world.

A SACRED DEATH

Nine years pass and a dear friend has just been diagnosed with terminal cancer. I would sit at her table each week with a cup of tea in a china cup and she would tell me stories. We would laugh together even in the face of a deeply painful and transforming time.

The weeks and months went by so quickly. I admired her greatly for not only her acceptance of something she could not control, but also her ability to still be graceful through all of her changes.

As we talk, I feel I should be there at the end of her life to support her daughters. She says she is okay with it but would have to discuss it with her daughters. This was to be the last time we spoke about it. I surrendered my thoughts about being there. If I was supposed to be there, I would be.

I don't see her in the couple of weeks leading up to her death. She is now too ill for visitors. I am sure that I have seen her for the last time.

On a dark starlit night, I wander outside into the paddock at home to say some prayers for my friend. I had been told the end was not far away so imagine my surprise when I 'see' her standing in front of me, vibrant red hair flaming behind her and wearing a highly polished suit of armour. Not what I am expecting. She shows herself to me as a Joan of Arc figure, a mighty warrior. I think that my friend is either close to passing or has indeed passed that night. I discover later that she had slipped into a coma that night.

The next day, I journey into my local town, thirty-five minutes' drive from home to run some errands. This is not a day I usually head into town but I am also meeting a friend for lunch and it is the only day we can get together.

After parking my car, I stand on the median strip for a few moments deciding which direction to head first. I make my choice and venture forward into my day.

Approaching my first destination, I come face to face with a woman I know and we just blink at each other for a moment before finally hugging. This is my friend's oldest daughter. She has just slipped into town to have a bit of a break she says and has only just arrived. Her mum has slipped into a coma and her passing won't be long now. I am invited to come and sit with my friend and say my goodbyes and also to spend time with her four daughters.

Spirit has conspired to get the two of us to meet in these unusual circumstances. What a blessing to be able to say goodbye to her.

I have said my goodbyes and drunk tea, laughed and cried with her daughters. I stand to leave and allow them to be with their grief. I am invited to stay longer. The talk and sharing of stories is a beautiful gift. I listen and hold the space for this time.

We all trundle into to my friend's bedroom to be with her, to share love with her. She looks so peaceful. Her bright red hair is magnificent. Her makeup is perfect and jewellery is in her ears. She looks as beautiful and graceful as always.

We sit, we talk, they sing to her and we wait. The girls move out of the room to talk and ask me to stay with her whilst they talk. Coming into the room once more, they ask me if I will stay with her until the end. They feel she won't go whilst they are still there. They say their loving goodbyes once more.

I am blessed to sit with my friend for another hour and a half until she herself decides it is time to go. I talk, tell her stories and offer some healing up for her. Peace permeates the room. I feel so blessed to have this very sacred time with her and her daughters.

A SACRED CROWNING

'Mum would like a reading please.'

These were the words that would awaken something beautiful in three women and take us all on a journey of self-acceptance, wonder and joy in the face of the bitch called terminal cancer.

I head out my front door to travel a short journey for our appointment. At the last minute something makes me grab my crystal crown. I don't know why, or if I will even bring her out of her calico travel bag but I trust this last-minute feeling as I always trust those subtle but powerful nudges.

Smiles and sadness greet me when I arrive at my destination. Love and laughter and tears are all to be a part of the journey this day. Three women, Mum, her loving daughter and I are held in the arms of the Goddess' embrace as we talk and stories are shared, where peace enters and sits beside us.

I sit opposite the beautiful woman whose journey is so harsh and reach for the bag I have brought with me. I talk about the Crone and how my journey is one of encouraging women to see her as worthy, as visible, as honoured.

Her first impressions are disbelief that the Crone could be thought of in such a way. The word Crone, like it is for so many, brings up images of the hag. Her loving daughter explains that my aim in life is to bring acceptance, visibility and respect to the Crone.

Taking the crystal crown from its bag, I ask permission to place it on her head and honour her as the Crone, the Wise Woman. The magic of this crown is palpable as I sit it upon her head. The shift in this fabulous Crone is evident on her face. Her beautiful face is animated as it moves from awe that this is happening to her, this honouring, to something akin to a light being switched on deep within her, deep within her soul. The light shining in her eyes seems to be one of remembering who she is beyond this mortal life. A sudden awareness of life beyond life perhaps.

A serene smile plays around her lips, her eyes hold a depth of wisdom that is almost impossible to describe in mere words. We sit in the beauty of this moment and she is the Queen, she is the Crone and she knows it and loves it.

I will never forget what I witnessed that day. It changed something in me too. It took me deeper than

I thought possible to honour women in rites of passage in some way.

The small acts of love and kindness that come just from trusting your intuition can make a huge difference in the lives of all involved. Never forget the beauty available when you do trust, even when life throws out the most horrendous of experiences. This day was one of grace, acceptance and something deeply profound.

Be aware of those gentle nudges coming from the other side. You just might make a difference in someone's life and your own life. We don't need to know the whole journey at the beginning. We need to trust the nudges that will lead us along the trails of life. This is the wow factor of life.

I was placed in situations where I was able to hold space… for a birth, a death and a sacred crowning, in my Crone years. I will never forget these journeys and the exceptional circumstances that led me to take them, to be able to be in the background whilst others did what needed to be done and do what was asked of me when needed. Trust is a big factor in life's journey. It is so often in the unusual circumstances that come to us that we see the most profound experiences. Our journey through life, when we become aware of these circumstances, will benefit all involved and not just self.

MESSAGES FROM THE CRONE

The journey through life is full of twists and turns. It is a road where trust becomes a measure of where you need to be, doing what needs to be done and who needs to be in your life. When the sacred road of the Crone is shown to you, will you follow it or turn away?

JOURNEY WITH THE CRONE

Spirit of my Crone, I honour you. In this time of sacred death and rebirth, this time of accepting my worthy crown, I am ready for this next and last sacred cycle. I understand now the power of the Crone as she emerges from deep within me. I am reborn into this sacred time in life where the spirit of the Crone is needed to bring about peace on earth. I am ready.

I am the Crone. I honour my sacred place in this time of life. I am at peace.

Build It and They Will Come

*L*IVING IN THE beautiful High Country of Victoria is a delight. We live on a mountain, surrounded by mountains, that is called a hill. We get several snowfalls in winter so I stubbornly call it a mountain. When I moved onto this mountain with my love, we cleared out old things that had no relevance to our new life and began our journey together with a blank canvas. The top four acres of land are flat (ish) and at that time, they were just paddocks with a house in the middle. The house is very cute but lacked colour and vibrancy. The potential for creation is strong in me and I was itching to splash some colour and vibrancy around.

The first thing I want to build on our property I say, is a labyrinth. I explain that a labyrinth is a unicursal path that leads you to your core, your centre and metaphorically speaking, back to source. As you journey around the labyrinth, you can invite healing energies to be with you, or ask for guidance, or focus on your footsteps as a way to welcome the quiet within. A walking meditation. You journey along its path through its many twists and turns. Sometimes you are walking near the centre before the path leads you away to the outer edges of the labyrinth. Finally, as you enter the centre space, you can rest awhile and discover the secrets of your soul's guidance held within the sacredness of the journey. What a great metaphor for life.

This spiral energy is something I have drawn on paper over and over again as a doodle, but it is also as a significant part of my Goddess work. To me the centre of the labyrinth and the centre of all of the spirals I create is representative of the spiritual path that we walk through life.

I do my research, find a pattern on the internet and give it to my love to draw up in the correct dimensions for me. I choose a place that has a cool, overhead canopy from the gum trees with views through other gums to the mountains beyond. He lays it out on the earth and in this sacred moment, my labyrinth is born. I move all of the rocks from other places around the property until my small singular path labyrinth is complete and I am happy. One of my long-held dreams has just been completed.

We are gifted some large rocks. It's one of those many times in life where you think about what you want and wallah, there it is. No effort involved. I wanted to create a sacred stone circle and here were the rocks, an offering from an outside source with no idea about me or my manifesting skills.

They were just a pile of large rocks for around eighteen months, grass growing high around them, a haven for snakes with many holes in which to hide. I awoke one day and said, today is the day we begin to create the Goddess circle. My love works out the dimensions required and the cardinal directions. A bobcat is needed to place them for us as they weigh so much more than it is possible for the two of us to move.

Twelve stones are laid around the edges of the circle and each stone is chosen to sit in a particular place. A central space is also dug for a firepit and the Goddess circle is born. Dust, barren earth, my stones and I am happy.

The rest of the stones are piled as I direct to create a rockery for plants near my stone circle. I am the only one who can see the vision for these sacred spaces. Over one year later and the grass has grown in and around the Goddess stone circle and my rockery, there are no hidey holes for snakes, and plants finish off the beautiful setting. My vision is now my reality. Sacred spaces created for ceremony and welcoming the Ancient Ones. Many Goddesses and Crones have arrived here for workshops, gatherings, ceremony and soul-nourishing days. Hold the vision and it will come when you least expect it and often in ways that go beyond your original vision.

I visioned these things over many years and surrendered them time and again as I could not logically see how they would manifest in my life. In my surrender I allowed space for everything to come together in one complete package. Trust is the key to successful creation.

MESSAGES FROM THE CRONE

You ask, we offer you a gift. What you do with that is as important as the gift itself. The gift may not look like what you asked for and yet, as you grow with it, as you build on it, it turns into something beyond your original request, beyond your expectations.

JOURNEY WITH THE CRONE

The earth is quiet. I hold my vision strong. I honour the East. The direction that will herald the birth of my vision. I honour the North. The direction that will ignite my passion for my vision. I honour the West. The direction that will allow me to divine each step I need to take in this sacred journey. I honour the South. The direction of earthing my vision in this physical realm. I come full circle. I am ready to create the reality of my vision.

I am the Crone. I honour my sacred place in this time of life. I am at peace.

Note: This is written for the Southern Hemisphere. In the Northern Hemisphere, reverse the directions of North and South.

Nature's Messengers and Gateway to the Crone

*N*ATURE OFFERS US hope, direction and confirmation about our journey. I have already written about Dragonfly; Nature's Shapeshifter and I am always aware that when something happens in unusual circumstances that I need to take notice.

The following story took place just after the full moon and a partial eclipse and culminated two weeks later with the new moon.

It is August and winter here in Australia. I am wondering about my direction, my mood reflective of the deeply introspective starkness of nature at this time.

When the events of nature offer more than a singular 'wow' event but a *series* of unusual events that insist I take notice, I instantly see the deeper meaning for me.

The first snow arrives around the time of the full moon eclipse; not an unusual event in itself. It is much later than usual but welcome here with its pristine beauty.

The following evening a beautiful pink fog rolls in and is filled with spirit orbs that are visible to the naked eye. Two nights later I step outside to see the Milky Way directly overhead, so vibrant and alive. As I stand marvelling at its clarity and beauty; a shooting star arcs across the sky.

Exactly one week after the full moon, I look out my door to see the end of a vibrant rainbow clearly visible in our paddock.

The new moon eclipse is another snowy and wind-fuelled day. I feel the shift within me that something magical and important is coming my way. My nights are filled with dreams, the energy is so intense.

The magic of the new moon eclipse fills me with hope and joy for my journey to come. Just days later I witness another end of a rainbow in our paddock. I know that all of these gifts from nature are showing me that something magical is awakening for me. Excitement fills the space where uncertainty was once present. I get it, I get the message loud and clear. Be patient. Something powerful is stirring.

Within weeks, I feel a nudge to create a gathering and ceremony and call it Gateway to the Crone. It is not something I consciously remember thinking, 'oh I need to create this event'. It just happens. Looking back to that time, I have no conscious recollection of how it unfolded.

By November I know that owl will be the totem for my Gateway to the Crone gatherings and ceremonies. Driving home one evening after a beautiful discussion about owl as my Gateway to the Crone totem, there she is, sitting on the side of the road. A Boobook owl, just a few km from home. Thinking she may be injured, I stop my car. She turns, takes off and flies across the bonnet of my car. A powerful confirmation indeed.

The first gathering and ceremony a few weeks later is a huge success. How could it not be, when everything I have been gifted by nature has told me that something magical was coming for me.

Five months after those first nature signs it is a warm summer evening and a dark moon. I stand in the inky darkness in my sacred stone circle sending out prayers of gratitude for Gateway to the Crone. I hear the distinctive call of my owl sister. The beautiful Boobook owl, the smallest owl. She is in the nearby gum trees. I finish my prayers. She stops her call. I stand silent in the deep introspective darkness of the night. A few moments of perfect peace and silence, and then, in the sacredness that is the magic of life, I feel the soft brush of a wing on my hair followed by three wing flaps and then, silence once more. I have just been gifted a powerful confirmation of my journey. A blessing for Gateway to the Crone and for me.

When you are open to the magic of life and the gifts that nature provides in unusual circumstances, it will light your way forward with openness and integrity without judgement and with the innocence of nature.

Mother Earth, the Goddess offered me the gifts that only nature can provide, messages that heralded the next steps on my journey. I am always grateful for the steps she shares with me, with love, from her heart to mine. It has always been this way, all of my life but I only consciously acknowledged her wisdom just twenty years ago.

MESSAGES FROM THE CRONE

When you look at nature as a gift, she will offer you messages that will take you on a journey of pure under-standing through the eyes of the Mother, the Goddess.

JOURNEY WITH THE CRONE

I sit silently under the big tree. You know the one. I remember it from so long ago. My back leans against the soft bark, her leaves hang low and embrace me in the green canopy. She is ancient, this sacred tree. She is wise and nurturing. I feel her in every part of me.

She knows me for I have climbed into her branches or leaned against her trunk many times over many years. I am the Crone now, in my own wise woman years. I rest against her, feeling her strength, her wisdom, her courage that comes from a long life lived anchored to this great earth. We are one, my sacred tree and I.

I am the Crone. I honour my sacred place in this time of life. I am at peace.

Come Sit at My Table

*S*ACRED RITUAL HAS been lost in a busy world. My aim is to see the return of the sacred ritual of tea making, cake and storytelling. I don't know why or when I started making this a conscious ritual. It was one of those natural things that evolved as I grew into my work with the Goddess and then with the Crone.

Reflecting back over my life, with no particular thought about the journey, an epiphany arrived into my musings. The ritual of tea, soul-nourishing food (AKA chocolate) and story listening with a pinch of wisdom sometimes added at the end has *always* been a part of my journey through life.

All of my adult life people have come to me when they need to be heard. They know I will keep their stories sacred, safe. They know I will listen without judgement and without interruption. They know they can tell me anything and I won't be shocked or send them away.

As they speak, I see their stories like a movie playing in my head. I thought everyone saw life this way.

It wasn't until I was in my early forties that I discovered I was clairvoyant. At that time, and in the many years to come, I always saw my life as pre-discovery and post-discovery. It was only when I was in my mid-fifties that I had one of those epiphanies and realised that I have *always* been clairvoyant and like so many, I had no idea about the spiritual nature of life.

When I reached the milestone of sixty and stepped fully into my work with Gateway to the Crone and began working ritualistically with teapots and beautiful cups and saucers and inviting women to 'come sit at my table' to share their stories, the last piece slotted into place.

I have worked this way through my whole adult life without conscious awareness. It was a training ground for when I came into my own as a 'Healer with Words' and began my Gateway to the Crone journey.

It was like I had long worked around the edges of who I was supposed to be, doing my passionate work but from the fringes of life rather in total immersion. It took a lifetime to reach down deep and unlock the door of my purpose, but the wait was worth the journey that was often filled with confusion and searching. We are never too old to remember why we came to this place at this time.

Looking back over a lifetime of lessons, challenges, highs and not so highs and lowest of lows, we see the pattern of our life emerging into our Crone cycle that expresses what we came here to do. I see that we are the culmination of a lifetime lived, survived and thrived. We are still here so we need to reflect on the past and present on occasion to discover the keys to the future.

Everyone should have 'come sit at my table' days. These are days where you get to be both the storyteller and the story listener. It is a gift to be able to be both.

MESSAGES FROM THE CRONE

The keys for your journey so often lie in the foundations of your past. Rather than discard the journey, look deeper at the stories emerging to create a bigger picture for your present and future journeying.

JOURNEY WITH THE CRONE

The passive nature of my journey is one of deep inner reflection. A time to look at the stories in life that showed me the way forward, each and every time. The stories that shaped me, even the ones I deemed as unworthy. I look into my heart and see a key, a sacred key that unlocks the next door of opportunity. I willingly grasp the key with both hands. I am ready to unlock the door that is now right of front of me. It is my time to shine as the spirit of the Crone.

I am the Crone. I honour my sacred place in this time of life. I am at peace.

A Rite of Passage

A RITE OF PASSAGE is something that shifts the energy from the ordinary to embracing the extraordinary. Gateway to the Crone was designed to honour the sacred Crone, to help her empower herself. These stories have been shared with permission from beautiful women who came to Gateway to the Crone for various reasons. For some, it is curiosity, some feel a pull, but all leave their ceremony feeling empowered and full of joy and hope for the future of the Crone and their own spirit of the Crone.

MICHELLE

I originally booked my day for Gateway to the Crone out of curiosity. I first envisioned a grizzled old Crone, bent over and bitter. Now I feel she is wise and beautiful, full of life's experiences, ready to share her knowledge with those willing to listen, available to assist those in need, powerful, radiant, wonderful, valuable. I am so glad to be in my Crone years now and know that my experiences in life can help others.

I love my Crone name of Maeve. It has a feeling of power and light. I use the name when I am wanting to lift myself, push past blocks, mainly creative blocks, to stand with me when I am standing my ground. I feel the power of Maeve, I feel more confident, supported, no longer alone. Aware that I am powerful and worthy. I loved wearing the crown as I made my Crone vows of intention. It was so uplifting and exciting.

I love thinking of myself as a Crone, as in ancient times, learned, wise, confident. I am speaking out more about the things I am passionate about, I have let go of 'stuff' I don't need.

My favourite part of the day was sitting at the table sharing our stories, being together in harmony and love. The day exceeded my expectations. I gained so much from the ceremony, from being with like-minded women and further exploring myself. I have gained self-confidence, new friendships and self-acceptance.

CAIREEN

When I thought about the word Crone, it reminded me of the witches in Macbeth. Old and outcast, relying on wisdom and ancient arts, shunned by society as one not to trust. I now know though, that the Crone is about learning to grow in grace with the wisdom of the Crone, being at peace and comfortable in my crone years. Saying farewell to the maiden, the mother and welcoming the Crone.

I was so nervous as I headed to this gathering and ceremony, finding myself driving and thinking should I turn around, what was I thinking. And then, I walked into a warm cosy gathering, the setting was above expectations, the vibe, love that word, was humming. I loved the very lady-like cups and saucers, the pretty sets, that we could choose where to sit. It was above what I expected. Memories of that day will be with me for a long time.

I love my Crone name Caireen. It honours who I have become on my journey through life, it has deep meaning to me. It is an honour, I think it chose me.

When the crown was placed upon my head in ceremony, I felt a wonderful sense of being in the moment and sharing my gratitude with the women surrounding me.

KIM

To me the word Crone conjured images of hags and witches and ugly old. Now I recognise my Crone identity as another part of me which bears the name Miriam. There is beauty and grace in the Crone now. I am in my sixth decade and it just felt right to recognise my age and celebrate it. I came to ceremony without expectations, so it was a surprising event, enlightening and empowering and I loved it.

I loved the drumming. It is like the heartbeat of the world and gives a sense of unity and oneness... it is so comforting and soothing. The tea making at the kitchen table reminds me of home and mother and sharing feelings and thoughts with others who care and can relate. There was a bubble of trust and honesty around us all in the gathering around the kitchen table. Although I have always found it hard to talk about my own story, in that setting I found I could.

The name Miriam confirms my Crone as a powerful and wonderful identity... Miriam fits like a glove... most of the time. Miriam comes into my mind more and more often, at times when I am feeling at a loss or sad and unsure. But also when I feel wonderful and energetic. That is my Miriam. I feel lighter and cannot help but smile when she is there. There is a sense of everything will be okay and is okay. It is very internally reassuring. It is as though I have a friend by my side at all times.

When the crown was placed upon my head in the ceremony, I initially felt a bit like an imposter or pretender but as the ceremony went on I felt more and more that I was in the right place, that I was given permission, that I was empowered to be this Crone Goddess.

I feel validated and happy in a very deep way. I realise there is more to me than I ever knew but I wasn't sure how to be more and now I have pride in my age and grateful to have achieved this age. I accept myself more and feel surer and more confident in myself and my decisions, most of the time.

Gateway to the Crone was one of the most powerfully validating events I have ever been to. I am so grateful to have attended. It has opened my glued shut mind eyes to a brighter, happier, more accepting sense of being. I am also beginning to feel more aware of the invisible world of spirit and lost family. They don't feel quite as lost to me now. Writing this has made me cry, at last.

SUE

I didn't like the word Crone. I always associated it with an old mean witchy woman. I feel great about it now I am the Crone, as I am not like that at all.

The rituals were wonderful. Tea making at the kitchen table took me back to my grandmother. At the table I shared a very hard story for me to tell about my depression and how it was not very nice. It was so hard to say those words but it has enabled me to move on from those days.

I received my Crone name and wondered if I had just made it up. The other names I heard around the table seemed more magical that my Moonbeam-Skye but on reflection that is the name I received, and I have always loved the moon and the sky, so I have really accepted my name now. When I speak my Crone name, I am calmer and ready to face anything that others throw at me.

I loved the feeling of the crown. I felt like a queen. My vows meant a lot to me as I knew I was going on to the next stage of my life. I know now I am a seer and I have a wonderful journey ahead of me.

JOY

When I heard the word Crone I didn't like and I still don't really, but when I heard about Gateway to the Crone I felt compelled to be there, a need to experience it. I didn't have any expectations but when I sat there with the other women, I found being with like-minded women was so uplifting. The ritual of tea making and drumming felt so emotional and yet empowering for me.

It was exciting for me to discover my Crone name and I use it often when I am outside looking up at the moon and the stars. I feel so uplifted in these times as a calm and stillness settles all around me.

The wearing of the crown in the ceremony made me feel strong and empowered. I have so much more belief and trust in myself now.

THE BEAUTIFUL WOMEN who have consented to have me share their experiences in entering the Gateway to the Crone, have explored so much about themselves in a new world. A world where the Crone is being more widely recognised as worthy, where she is becoming more visible and seen as a valuable asset for her wisdom.

The Crone, in her self-acceptance is shining her light from a place of determination to live her dreams, to make her mark in a new way in this world. She is ready to identify herself as Crone, a Wise Woman and share herself with those who seek her wisdom, her stories, her rituals.

It is in the sacredness of ritual and a rite of passage ceremony and the gathering of women for story-weaving that I see women understanding their worth, understanding the journey of the Crone, and feeling the power inherent in opening the crown of deep wisdom. The symbolism held within the tools with which we work to create change, has the ability to flick a switch within the heart and soul of the Crone.

MESSAGES FROM THE CRONE

The connectedness of the Crone in all her glory, her wisdom, her pain, her sorrow, her joy creates a wise woman connecting with other wise women. The journey of the Crone is one of remembering who she is and being a beacon of light for others to journey alongside of her. Such is the way of the Crone.

JOURNEY WITH THE CRONE

I dig deep, wondering about my journey into the wilds of the unknown Crone. I hesitate to honour her, remembering the stories of the hag, the witch.

I close my eyes and see a woman, a beautiful aging woman walking towards me, a smile playing about her sensuous lips. I hear in my mind and in my heart, I am the spirit of the Crone. I will guide you well in these aging years. I will hold your hand and walk beside you, showing you the way forward, with love in your heart for the wise woman that you truly are.

I will help you remember your stories, remember the journey of being in your power time as a Crone. This is a sacred time in your life. We walk together, in vibrancy and joy, encouraging peace to walk with us now. You are the Crone. You are worthy of knowing your beauty in these sacred years. Be strong, be courageous and honour me, the spirit of the Crone. I am you, you are me. We are one.

I am the Crone. I honour my sacred place in this time of life. I am at peace.

PART TWO

The Modern Crone

The Crone's Toolkit, Invocations,
Mini Ceremony, Affirmations,
Dancing, Dreaming, Recipe,
Meditations, Creating

*I*MAGINE... A WOMAN with dreams. Her life experiences have, at times, brought her to her knees and still she walks on. Still she knows that she can make it through another day, another hour. Still she knows to never give up on her dreams. Her dreams may have shifted and changed over these many years, but they are still vibrant and alive. She has achieved so much and she is excited by this new phase in her life. She wraps some new dreams around her, ready now to accept she is worthy of achieving them.

The modern Crone is often still working, still raising a family or caring for grandchildren or elderly parents. She has traversed menopause and the shifts that come with aging. As she ages, life often attempts to render her invisible in a youth driven world and yet, she still never gives up.

The modern Crone steps into her power time, an awakening of a sensual, deeply feminine and sexual time. If only she permits herself to explore this deeply primal nature of herself.

A modern Crone explores new avenues for creative expression, she takes no BS from those around her. Her stories, her dreams, her goals may change shape as she ages, but they are valid dreams and are rightfully explored.

A modern Crone is ready for the next adventure. Bring it on, she declares!

THE MODERN CRONE is someone who is ready to embrace the unknown, who is willing to die to the old ways of living life, who is ready to take on a new adventure, who is a dreamer and yet practical, who is a seer who sees beyond the ordinary, a healer who heals by showing the way, a Wise Woman who speaks the truth, as she sees it, when needed and not a moment before.

The modern Crone is deeply feminine and expresses herself through her manner, her proud carriage as she ages, who speaks her mind and follows her dreams. The modern Crone is alive and well and ready to show the world her mettle, her vibrant and colourful nature.

In this section you will explore fun Crone tools for the journey, incantations, invocations, awakenings, self-exploration, colour work, dream-weaving and journey stone creation to embrace the modern Crone within.

The Crone's Toolkit

❖ **Crown** ~ Essential for any Crone toolkit. It can be metaphorical *or* one you have created or were drawn to bring into your Crone life.

❖ **Teapot, Teacups & Saucers** ~ Include some sacred herbal teas and you are ready for the perfect 'Come sit at my table' ritual.

❖ **20 cm Round Cake Tin** ~ and a simple tea cake recipe (see page 147 for recipe). A quick whip up when your Crone sisters drop by for a story-weaving session or when someone needs your story listening skills.

❖ **Sage** ~ or other cleansing herb or plant to keep your sacred Crone space clear of outdated patriarchal and societal ideals about the Crone.

❖ **Sacred Bowl or Basket**~ wooden, pottery, stone or woven perhaps. This represents the sacred womb of the Wise Blood.

❖ **Candles** ~ Essential in any tool kit for doing magical workings. Deep red, green, gold, natural or any colour that resonates with you.

❖ **Oversized Fluffy Towels** ~ Luxury is a gift well deserved by the Crone after a sacred bath or shower or perhaps dancing in the rain.

❖ **Bubble Bath** ~ to soak in a sacred bath filled with yummy aromatic bubbles. *Or*, perhaps you prefer the alcoholic kind of bubbles to sip as you soak.

❖ **Chocolate** ~ One should always have at least one block of chocolate in her pantry for emergency story-weaving sessions and personal satisfaction.

❖ **Outdoor Cauldron** ~ Perfect for your sacred *soul fire* for ceremony *and* it is also wonderful those sensual evenings of pleasure, with self or a loved one. Think bubbles (the drinking kind) and toasted marshmallows by the fire.

❖ **Altar** ~ A place for sacred Crone magical tools.

❖ **Sexy Lingerie** ~ At least one sexy item of clothing and/or lingerie. One needs to feel the luxury of a sensual garment clinging to one's skin seductively.

❖ **Gypsy Skirt** ~ At least one for those swirling, twirling dance steps. Dance like *everyone* is watching!

❖ **Bling Anklet & Toe Ring** ~ and seductive nail polish for your toes. Essential for the barefooted Crone as she wanders barefoot on the earth to connect with the Goddess.

❖ **Big Tinkly Earrings** ~ to remind you to play.

❖ **Power Lipstick** ~ In a colour that enhances those seductive lips.

❖ **Attitude** ~ Find your sassy. Walk with feminine strides, swing those hips (where aging stiff hips allow that is) with a smile like you have a delicious secret written all over your glorious Crone face.

THIS IS ONLY the beginning. Add to your Crone toolkit *anything* that feels good for you. The rise of the Crone is also the rise of the sacred wise feminine spirit. You will always know what your Crone wants as she nudges you to create fun and laughter and joy in these beautiful powerful years of the Wise Blood.

Some irreverence in a dull world is necessary to lift the Crone spirit above the mundane.

Sacred Sensual Crone

*T*HIS SELF-EXPLORATION JOURNEY is one of sensual sensory and primal pleasure. This is a self-exploration exercise so it is something to experience for yourself however, if you have a partner, you may also want to share this time with them.

What you will need:

❖ An hour or two of your time when you will not be disturbed.

❖ Diffuser and essential oils… A sensual blend or your favourites that evoke a sense of peace and readiness to explore… I love the ancientness of Frankincense… or a favourite incense.

❖ Something sacred and feminine to wear… a satin bathrobe perhaps or silky lingerie or flowing dress.

❖ Chocolate optional.

❖ Bubbles or favourite wine or tea along with a beautiful glass or cup.

❖ Sacred food that nourishes your body and soul.

❖ Massage oil.

❖ Music to create the sensual mood.

❖ Bath or shower.

❖ Candles – lots of them if possible and matches or a lighter.

❖ Two soft fluffy towels in a colour that speaks to your sensual soul. For example, soft pink for love, red for passion or green for harmony or whatever colour appeals to you.

Intuitively find your sacred space in which to weave your sensual magic. Choose a time where you will not be disturbed. Look around your room and move anything that feels discordant with this sensual journey.

Place candles in safe receptacles around the room. Feel where you should place each candle for maximum light and benefit. Light your candles.

Place your diffuser and oils or incense in position in readiness and switch on or light.

Drape your item of clothing elegantly on a chair or bed.

Place the chocolate, bubbles, wine or teapot and cup on a table close by.

Have some ambient music playing in the background.

In the bathroom lay out your two soft fluffy towels. Place the massage oil on the side of the bath or table. Place a candle in a safe receptacle on the side of the bath or a table and light as you run your warm bath or prepare to take a luxurious shower.

Discarding your everyday clothes, sink into your bath or step under your shower. You can hear the music playing in the background. The candle beside you is flickering lazily in time to the mood being set. Take as long as you need to enjoy the warm sensuality of water playing over your naked body.

When you are ready step out of the water and pick up one of your fluffy towels. Wrap it around you and slowly dry your body beginning at your feet and ankles and working your way up your body.

Take your massage oil and place a little in the palm of your hand. Beginning again at your feet and ankles, massage the luxurious oil into your body, moving with slow and sensuous movements. Take your other fluffy towel and pat down your body of excess oil.

Walk naked to the room in which your candles are burning seductively. Take your item of clothing and let it slip effortlessly over your body, clinging to your slightly damp curves with the feeling of luxury.

Sit on your couch or bed and pour yourself your bubbles or wine or tea and sip slowly. Take a piece of chocolate and let it melt in your mouth. Close your eyes and breathe in the aromas of your essential oils. The music is calling to you to dance. You rise and begin to sway to the music feeling light on your feet. You are immersed in a meditative space. Your sensual nature has been aroused by this gift of sacred and sensual time, just for you.

The rest of the journey now is only limited by your imagination as you take pleasure in this sensual sensory journey. Enjoy the pleasures this journey can bring to your life and take that pleasurable feeling of wellbeing into your everyday life. Take as long as you need to enjoy the journey. When you are ready to emerge back into your everyday world, smile a secret smile of joy at your awakened sensual being as you pack away the journey until next time. No-one needs to know all of your beautiful journey!

The more you offer yourself this sacred gift, the more peace and joy and pleasure will be a part of your journey, even in the everyday world.

Awaken Your Creative Spirit

*T*HIS IS AN incantation and ritual to work with when you are ready to move through any perceived energy blocks and awaken your creative spirit. This is a time to awaken the magic of your spirit, to create something in your life, that can lead you away from dark perceptions and into the light of creation.

This incantation is working directly with your spirit. The power of the spoken words carrying on the winds of change to create change in your life in a positive way.

Creativity comes in many forms, not just writing and art. It might be in your everyday life, in your workplace, with your children, in your garden or your kitchen. There are no limits to how the creative spirit will help us on our journey through life.

This incantation is written for the Southern Hemisphere and in the Northern Hemisphere swap the words North for South and South for North.

What you will need:

❖ Sage or gum leaves to cleanse you and your space and a fire proof container.

❖ 30 minutes and a special place where you will not be disturbed.

❖ Orange candle and matches or a lighter.

❖ Creative spirit incantation.

∽ INCANTATION ∽

My creative spirit
Awakens in me…
The Goddess of change
Is *my* sacred key.
The East is my muse…
Her vision is bright.
The creative spark welcome…
In the dawn of new light.
The North is my passion…
My journey is fire.
Igniting my spirit…
With a courageous desire

The West is for seeing…
The water to divine.
My spirit held reflective…
Her creation sublime.
The South is my elder…
My earth is my ground.
I anchor my spirit…
To assure her she is sound.
My within is my Goddess…
She walks with me now.
I honour this trail…
This *is* my sacred vow.

Taking your sage or gum leaves, matches or a lighter, a fireproof bowl and your orange candle and holder and incantation and enter your sacred and quiet space. You may already have created an altar space for magical workings.

Place your candle in front of you and light it, honouring the sacredness of the flame and the colour orange, the colour to guide the awakening of your creative spirit.

Place your sage or gum leaves in your fireproof bowl and light. Once they are flaming, blow on them gently so that you now have fragrant smoke. Moving the bowl around your body, beginning at your feet and passing the bowl around you, let the smoke drift around you.

As you work around your body say,

'Sacred smoke carry away anything negative from my being now.'

Once you have finished with your sacred smudge, carefully move around your space to cleanse the space for this awakening of your creative spirit.

When you have finished, place your bowl alongside your candle and make yourself comfortable, holding the incantation on your lap.

Take three deep breaths and release them with a sigh. Focus on your breath, allow it to become steady and rhythmic.

Look into the flame of your orange candle and invite the Crone to be with you now, to guide your journey to awakening your creative spirit. You may already be working with your creative spirit, but you may have come across a creative block and this incantation will assist you in moving forward on your creative journey.

Feel your heartbeat beat in time with the heartbeat of the spirit of the Crone . Hear your breath as it slowly rises and falls in your body.

You are ready.

Take your incantation and begin to read with feeling. Pace the words. As you read, feel in your body where you feel your awakening creative spirit or where the blocks are held and are beginning to move now.

When you finish the incantation, take a few moments to pause and feel the words and their meaning and the stirring of your creative spirit within you. Read it twice more, each time feeling it deeper and deeper within you.

When you have finished reading the incantation aloud the third time, sit and look into the flame of your candle for a few more moments. Honour the journey with the Crone as your mentor.

You will feel the energy of this time recede as you bring your focus back into your space in present time.

You can work with this incantation as often as required to move blocks or to awaken your creative spirit for a particular project.

Words are powerful. Feel your awakened creative spirit stirring in your life, guiding you on to new adventures and projects.

Extinguish your candle. Make sure your sage or gum leaves are completely extinguished. Place your incantation alongside your candle and allow the energy to keep flowing long after you have entered the realm of the everyday once more.

Acceptance

WORK WITH THESE words as an affirmation, a mantra, to shift the spirit of the Crone into a higher place of self-acceptance. When we repeat affirmations, incantations, mantras, we move any perceived blocks to our Crone spirit.

Write your own mantras. Take a pen and paper, rather than working on or near a computer. Walk out in nature and perhaps sit under a favourite tree.

Take three deep breaths and release them with a sigh, settling into your nature-filled space with love. Call on the Crone to guide your pen this day so that you may write your own affirmation or mantra.

Sit quietly in this space until you feel your creative spirit bubble up within you and encourage you to put pen to paper. Let the energy flow without attempting to push it.

If you find you cannot write on your first attempts, create a time where you can visit the same place again and again, setting your intention to write for yourself.

In this sacred place in nature read the following mantra/affirmation aloud to encourage the flow of your Crone spirit to rise higher and higher.

When you feel the energy return to nature, offer a thank you to your space and to the Crone and return to your everyday life. Visit as often as you feel the call to write your affirmations.

I am the light... I am the Crone...

I am the dark... I am the Crone...

I am no longer held prisoner in a world of
    disconnection... of invisibility...

I seek my joy... on the highest of peaks...

I seek my worth... in the depths of my
    inspired life...

I am love... I am bliss... I am the word...
    the story... the beginning and the end...

I am reborn... a Goddess... a Crone
    Goddess...

The lines upon my face... visible tracks of
    my life... reflections of a life lived to the
    best of my ability...

The trails I now walk… are as deep and
meaningful… as those trails well-trodden
by the Ancients who guide me now…
I am the light…
I am the dark…
I am the Crone…
Watch me now…

Create Your Own
Journey Stones

SMOOTH RIVER OR OCEAN WASHED ROCKS FOR STORY-WEAVING AND HAG STONES FOR FOCUS

Stones are called the record keepers of the earth and therefore working with them in such a sacred way, is an honour to them. Stones are like working with an old friend. They are ancient, having been here since the beginning of the earth's formation.

A journey stone created by the hands of the Crone, is a tangible reminder of the things in life that are being created for the good of the Crone. I see your journey stones as tangible reminders for remembering your journey.

To me it is more a symbol of remembering the good journey through life. It is about setting your intentions for it and placing your own considerable Crone energy within it, almost like a storage device to be activated when needed.

Or perhaps telling your new chapter into your life story to the stone as a reminder of what you are creating every time you wear it or see it.

You can also create these stone record keepers as a story stone. A place to speak your own old sacred stories as they bubble up into the surface of your consciousness in readiness to be released.

You will need:

❖ A smooth small river rock or a hag stone. A hag stone is a stone usually gifted from the ocean or a river in which there is a naturally forming hole.

❖ Paint pens or similar to draw or write on your stones.

❖ If you are working with a hag stone, a leather thong to be able to wear it.

❖ If you are working with a hag stone for wearing, you may also like to choose to add beads or feathers or crystals to your necklace.

WORKING WITH A SMALL RIVER STONE

You will find that a stone calls to you in nature. I have so often 'heard', pick me as I walked the edges of the oceans and rivers. Ask the spirits of the area if it is right for you to take home this stone and trust your intuition. Stones from the ocean or rivers or waterfalls are often perfect for this journey.

Your stone is already charged with its own record keeper journey as well as its journey within water or earth. Therefore, if the stone has chosen you, it wants to work with you in your creation of a new chapter.

When you get your stone home, take out your paint pens or paints.

Sit with your stone in your hands in the quiet of your space and think about your journey now and what you are creating. Meditate on your journey and ask the spirit keeper of the stone for symbols that need to be painted on the stone.

Symbols are the language of the soul and will hold meaning to you for this Crone journey. It also could be a word rather than a symbol. Trust the journey.

Paint these symbols or words on the surface of your stone.

Carry this stone with you in your pocket or your bra perhaps as a tangible reminder of the beauty you are creating in your life. Sit in meditation with your stone whenever you feel the pull to do so and listen to the stories held within the stone for the journey ahead.

The energy you pour into your journey stone will be reciprocated with assistance for the journey. The energy of your journey becomes stronger because of what you put into it.

WORKING WITH A HAG STONE

It is said that looking through the hole of a hag stone is a view into the world of the faeries. It is also said to be a stone for healing and protection. To me, when you look through the naturally formed hole, it focuses your view to a narrow point and is a tangible reminder to focus on your creative intent rather than becoming distracted with the extraneous happenings.

As you walk near the ocean, she may offer up a hag stone to you. When I lived down on the coast of the Southern Ocean, she gifted me many which I, in turn, have gifted to others.

When you receive your gift of a hag stone, you may like to wear it as a pendant as a tangible reminder to focus your intent on your creations on your Crone journey.

Your hag stone is already charged from its long journey in the ocean. When it appears for you, it is a gift from the spirits of the ocean.

Take your leather thong and make a loop with it through the natural hole in your stone. It is ready to wear. Alternatively, you may also like to add feathers, shells or other adornments on your necklace.

Whenever you feel the cool of your stone around your neck, or an energy shift within the stone, it is a reminder to take a look through the hole and metaphorically see your journey and what you need to focus on in this moment.

Dancing in the Wild
Woman Crone

*D*ANCE, MUSIC AND song are keys to unlocking the creative wild woman spirit of the Crone. It is easy to get caught up in the pain of aging and a lack of vibrancy because we live in a youth driven world. It is time to change the status quo and be seen... be vibrant... be alive...

Being irreverent and not caring what others think is important. Dancing, singing, painting, writing, creating is important. Being inspired by shifting the energy of the Crone from one state of sluggish energy into another is called alchemy, and alchemy is important.

Dance certainly is one of the key ingredients to spiritual or Crone alchemy. If the energy of the moment is depleting your Crone spirit of its vibrancy then playing with dance, music and song is the answer to reigniting your passion for life. You are literally dancing in the Crone.

I love to dance outside on the grass or inside my home if the weather is inclement. Choose a place where you will be free to dance wildly, like the wild woman you are meant to express and to sing at the top of your lungs.

You will need:

❖ A favourite piece of music… that uplifts your soul, makes your heart sing and gets your feet and body moving with the rhythm.
❖ Candles – create a circle of candles or shells or stones to build up the vibration of the Crone spirit.
❖ Nature.

Wear something flowing and feminine.

Keep your feet bare.

Before turning on your music… say a little prayer of welcome to the spirits of the music… The sylphs… the air spirits. They love music of all kinds (okay maybe not heavy metal).

For example:

Dear spirits of the air, please hear my music with the love I offer you now as we dance together in harmony.

Or write your own prayer of gratitude.

Set your scene for this dance, whether it is tribal, or classical or anything in between, it is important to create a beautiful and energetic sacred space in which to dance. You may choose to set up a circle of candles and light them. Ensure they are in a safe receptacle and a safe distance from where you intend to dance so they will not be knocked over. Or perhaps choose to create a circle of stones or shells. This is a sacred space in which to welcome and embrace the vibrant Crone energies through glorious dance moves. Remember that your choice of music and dance moves are personal and the spirits of the air will love them. Begin with some sacred music in the background whilst you set your intention to dance up a storm! Your intention, your music and your dance will cleanse this sacred space of any unwanted and negative energies.

Stand in the centre of your circle and say the following incantation out loud and in a sing-song voice three times.

As you speak turn slowly around in your dancing circle and feel the rise of the Crone energies.

⟿ INCANTATION ⟿

My feet are ready dance…
My soul ready to receive…
There is a song in my heart… a story…
A story… I am ready to weave…
My voice is loud and strong…

I sing to the sky above…
I stomp my feet to a sacred rhythm
Likened to a sacred drum…
The heartbeat of Mother Earth…
I feel her beneath my feet…
The song of power I remember now…
I am fuelled by a compelling heat…
I stop for a moment
And fall to the earth…
My soul is now at peace…
The spirit of the Crone…
Is a spark ignited…
With the greatest love…
Crones are now united.
I dance my dance…
To the rhythm of earth's song…
I sing her sacred words…
My beating heart is strong…
The rhythm of my life…
Shows the vibrant way…
To dance in the Crone
Is to welcome a new day.

When you have finished speaking, stand quietly in the centre of your circle for a few moments and feel the gentle acceleration of these vibrant energies. The sylphs are with you as the pace now picks up speed.

Turn your favourite piece of music up loud and feel the vibrancy reverberate throughout your body. Let your feet begin to move without trying to force the flow. Your body will begin its fluid movement as you dance around your sacred dancing circle. Immerse yourself in the music and the beat as your body, your mind, your heart and your soul are one with the flow of life. Sing out loud to the music. Be at one with the music.

The wild woman is present, the Crone is awake and alive with the vibrancy of life. Keep dancing and singing as long as you feel the energy.

When you are finished, slow down the pace and sway to the music. Turn down the volume and play something gentle.

You have released your inner wild woman, you have danced in your Crone. You are ready to show the world just how vibrant and alive and visible you truly are now.

Extinguish your candles and deactivate your sacred circle by putting away the sacred items used to create your circle. That dance and circle are alive within you now as you head into your day, as you embrace a new chapter in the life of your Crone spirit.

Dance as often as you feel you would like. Nature's dancefloor is your key to unlocking and igniting the wild woman within, the key to dancing in your Crone.

Invite Love into Your Life

LOVE COMES IN many forms and I have found that many say to me, I am not sure I know what love feels like. When the heart has been wounded, blocks can be placed in the heart as protection against future hurt and the heart feels shut down to love.

I see the importance of self-love first and all other love can flow from that seed of self-love. Yes, we may be hurt again through loss, but sometimes we need to take a chance on love and bask in the glow of self-love. Those very words, 'bask in the glow of self-love' can make you feel uncomfortable.

I see that we are a work in progress in so many areas of our life and that is fabulous because if we didn't know the low times, how could we possibly know just how high we can reach.

The sacred Crone has fallen over many times on her journey through life and been hurt and this is where I feel that self-love can be the key to transitioning into feeling the depth of what is possible with loving self.

I wrote the following affirmation many years ago, when I was in the depths of self-loathing. I stuck it on my bathroom mirror and made myself say it every day, at least once a day and then every time I went into the bathroom. It took a while for me to look at myself in the mirror and yet, over time, I finally came to a place of self-acceptance and the self-love came later.

Learning to love self creates a deeper love and appreciation for those around you, the environment, the Goddess. It takes as little or as long as it takes. There is no time limit for this self-love gig. It is so often a life-long process and this is a starting point.

Work with this affirmation first or create your own in your own sacred words. Words carry power when spoken aloud. It is a powerful journey.

⤚ WHEN I LOOK IN THE MIRROR ⤚

When I look in the mirror
I see beauty.
Life vitality emanates from *every* part of me.

My eyes glow clearly with soul knowledge
My heart beats strongly with soul love.
Peace settles gently through me;
Happiness is like a beacon shining from my
    core.
I tenderly forgive myself
For the destruction I have placed on my
    being
And vow that today;
Today
I begin my journey home!

Abundance Mini Ceremony

WHAT THIS CEREMONY MEANS TO YOU

This ceremony is to assist you in attracting more abundance into your life. This may be financial abundance, an abundance of love, of peace or anything at all. When you perform this ceremony be clear in your intention, however also leave room in your life to attract the abundance you need rather than just the abundance you want. You may ask for more abundance however you may first need to recognise that abundance comes in many forms. This ceremony is designed to be only one facet of your abundance journey.

What you will need:

❖ Green, white or gold candle.

❖ Sage (usually available from health food or new age shops) or gum leaves.

❖ Matches to light your candle and sage.

❖ Candle holder or similar for your candle.

❖ Fireproof dish for your sage.

❖ Stones, shells, crystals or similar to create a sacred circle of power.

1. Perform this ceremony when you are feeling balanced and grounded.

2. Place stones, crystals, shells or whatever feels right for you to create a sacred circle in a special place to you. Create the circle big enough for you to sit or stand in. Make sure you perform this ceremony at a time and place where you will not be disturbed. (*Note*: I find sunrise or sunset really powerful times).

3. Taking your candle and smudge and any tools with which you wish to work, enter your circle from the East direction as this is the direction of new beginnings and new personal growth. Walk counter clockwise (Southern Hemisphere) or clockwise (Northern Hemisphere) and find the position in your sacred circle that feels right for you to sit or stand for this abundance ceremony.

4. Place your candle in a safe receptacle in the centre of your circle and light.

5. Place your sage leaves in your fire proof receptacle (e.g. abalone shell or similar) and light. Blow gently until the leaves are smoking rather than flaming. Move around your circle and fan the smoke around the circle with your free hand or a special feather, and then move the receptacle up your body and around your body. The sage leaves are to be worked with to clear your circle and yourself energetically in readiness for your ceremony.

6. Say the following as you move around your circle with your sage smoke: 'I willingly release anything that is not energetically compatible with my intention to welcome more abundance into my life.' Place the receptacle on the ground near your candle & allow it to extinguish by itself.

7. Now sit comfortably and take a few moments to take three deep breaths as you relax your mind and body. Imagine yourself at peace with your environment. Take a few more moments to feel the power of your sacred space within your circle.

8. Imagine a powerful golden light embracing you and your sacred circle for protection.

9. The following three aspects of your ceremony are to be spoken out loud as you declare your intention

to create abundance in your life. Your words carry immense energy.

∞ INVOCATION ∞

I ask only for that which is for my highest
good to come to me today.
I honour and invoke the Goddess, beautiful
Earth Mother and the spirit of the Crone
as my witness to creating an abundant life.
I invite the divinely feminine power of
the Goddess to flow around me and fill
me with her abundant love, power and
strength.
I honour the sanctity and sacredness of all
life. I honour the great circles and cycles
of life as they flow to me. I honour the
cycles of life – birth, life, death and rebirth.
I honour the daily cycles of life.

*Take a few quiet moments to feel and experience the
wonderful energies of ceremony.*

∞ GRATITUDE PRAYER ∞

Note: Gratitude for what you already have in your
life attracts more of what you want into your life.

I am grateful for the beauty in my life;

The people; my home and even the lessons that
have helped me grow into my personal truth.

I am grateful for my divine connection to
Mother Earth.

I am grateful for my sacred guides.

I am grateful for my intuitive and creative
self.

My life is *my* journey and I am grateful for
the adventures my soul guides me to
take on that journey.

I am truly blessed to live my life to its
fullest potential.

Be silent for a moment and think your own gratitude thoughts.

∼ INTENTION ∼

*This is your declaration of your intention to create abundance
in your life.*

I, (insert your name) set my intention to create abundance in my life. I recognise new ways of welcoming and living with abundance. I *accept* abundance as *my divine right* in *every* area of my life.

I now take powerful and positive steps forward to successfully create lasting abundance. I willingly follow the positive signposts that require action on my part to step firmly into this sacred time in my life.

I welcome this new abundance into my life. I understand that abundance begins with my own belief that I am *deserving* of a new wave of abundance to assist me on my life journey.

I *am* ready to accept abundance into my life. I understand that abundance will always come to me in ways that I *need* and recognise that my needs will *always* be met.

Any further intentions you would like to personally add may be declared at this time!

Note: Abundance does not always arrive as a financial consideration. When you ask for abundance it may arrive as an abundance of knowledge or wisdom that will assist you to earn financial abundance. It may be an abundance of good friends who offer their loving support. Notice the abundant signposts of your life journey as they appear and remember to hold gratitude for your abundance in whatever form it arrives.

At the completion of your vows of intention, you may like to take a few minutes to be silent and really feel the wonderful intensity of what you have just stated. You may also like to write your feelings, thoughts and inspirations in a journal to reflect on at a later time as abundance comes to you. Keeping a record of this powerful journey will keep your faith in the journey strong!

COMPLETION OF CEREMONY

Sit quietly and imagine/visualise your intention being sent outward from you to be made manifest in your life. Do not be fixed on time frames, or the ways you 'think' your abundance will arrive, or exactly what your abundance will be.

Once you have declared your intention for more abundance in your life, surrender it and let it come to you naturally without pushing for it, before it is ready to arrive. Be aware of your intuitive feelings that say that you must put certain actions into place or when you feel the need to be quiet, honour that as well. Trust in your process of creation and follow your intuitive feelings.

This journey now is about moving forward into a new stage in your life.

Give thanks to your angels, guides, the Crone and the Goddess for being with you in ceremony and bearing witness to your declaration of intent. Your prayers have been heard.

It is time to leave your sacred circle. Extinguish your candle and leave via the East direction again. Your ceremony is complete.

Notice the positive changes happening within you and around you.

Collect your stones or crystals etc. You may like to keep them specially for ceremony as stones hold the memories of what you are creating.

Enjoy your ceremony and welcome the energy of abundance into your life with an open mind and a loving heart.

Dream-Weaving the Crone Journey

*D*AY DREAMS, NIGHT dreams are all inspired imaginings coming from your guidance to help you on your journey through life.

Dreams hold symbols that are the language of the soul. Differentiate between the dreams of ordinary regurgitated events of the day and those that hold a powerful message. There is a vibrancy to them. I often find that my most powerful dreams are the ones just before I wake up in the morning.

There is an added vibrancy to your power dreams. They are so often filled with colour and detail and symbols for the journey. Dreaming symbolically ensures that you will remember the uniqueness of your dream. It is in the unravelling of the detail of your dream, that you will remember it and apply it to your life.

What you will need to encourage your night-time power dreams:

❖ A deep blue candle in a safe receptacle.

❖ Matches or lighter.

❖ Prayer for invoking power dreams.

❖ Journal and pen.

❖ Diffuser and essential oils to evoke good dreaming. I like Frankincense, Jasmine and Sandalwood or research oils you like to diffuse for dreaming.

Remove any technological devices from your bedroom. You are creating a calm and peaceful atmosphere in which to welcome a powerful dream. Call the spirit of the Crone to be with you as you dream. Turn off your harsh main light and have a lamp with a soft coloured globe or shade as your light.

Place your journal and pen and your prayer on your nightstand.

Light your deep blue candle in a safe place whilst you make your preparations.

Have a safe diffuser in your bedroom and place three drops of your favourite oil blend into the diffuser.

Sit on your bed and begin to focus on your breath. Take three deep breaths, releasing each with a sigh. As you breathe in, you are welcoming relaxation and positive energy into every part of you. As you breathe out, you are releasing anything unwanted and unneeded at this time. Allow your breath to become slow and steady. Let the thoughts come and go without attempting to stop them. Feel yourself relax into this sacred space you have created.

When you feel yourself relaxing, say the following prayer or one you have written yourself.

⸙ PRAYER ⸙

I invite my dreams to guide my way
through life. They are sacred to my
journey. I invite my power dreams to be
vibrant and alive with possibilities for the
journey ahead. I embrace them with love.
They are positive reflections of my journey
and offer direction when I need guidance.
I invite the Crone to be my guide as I
journey in my slumber. I am well protected
in my night-time journeying. I remember
my dreams in detail. I understand the
symbols offered within my dream state.
Each dream is a chapter to add to my
journey as a sacred Crone. I welcome my
power dreams with a loving embrace.

Extinguish your candle before going to bed. If you do not dream on the first attempts, keep the ritual going each night you wish to dream. The energy is building for the dreams to come when you ask.

When you do dream the power dreams, turn on your light and write the dreams in detail in your journal. If you get out of bed and do something else first, the essence of the dream is likely to be lost.

Write everything you can remember and write the date of the dream at the top of the page. Over time, your dreams will create a story that will guide your Crone journey. Enjoy your dreams. They are glimpses into the worlds beyond this world that offer powerful insights into your Crone journey.

Colour is the New Black

WHO SAYS CRONES have to wear black? It is something that appears to be associated with the Crone, the witch, the hag. I see that colour is the new black!

Crones are vibrant, full of life. They love to dance and stand proud in their aging bodies. They wear vibrant colours and colour their hair in bright colours.

For many Crones it is no longer the boy-shaped cut of the hair, trousers and oversized shirts and sensible shoes. I see a shift in the Crone persona. I see that she is growing her hair longer or creating more stylish and flattering ways of wearing her beautiful crowning glory.

I see more Crones wearing dresses and skirts or jeans with sexy tops and big earrings. I see them shining their colours from the inside out. I see the healing colours bringing out the vibrancy of the Crone in a sometimes-dull world. Go Crones!!

LET'S BRING OUT THE PRACTICAL CRONE FOR A MOMENT (OKAY SO MAYBE AN HOUR OR TWO)

Open the door to your wardrobe and pull everything out. Yes, I mean *everything*! Look at everything lying there on your bed and floor. Touch the fabrics, feel the colours. When did you last wear it? How did you feel when you wore it?

What feels good? What serves you in your everyday life? What is for cleaning the house and what meets your needs for going to work?

Now look at the overall colours you wear and the different colours for different occasions. Do you want to feel more vibrant at work but wear classic black most of the time? Add colour. Do you hate doing the housework and so wear your oldest daggiest clothes? Add something vibrant and dance whilst you work.

If you spend most of your everyday life in drab colours that don't make you zing (yes that's a word), then bring more colour into your everyday world. Why spend most of your day in drab, when you could be a colourful and outrageous Crone who gets noticed for all the right reasons.

Now put back the clothes than make you zing and give away the rest. If you are now standing naked in the middle of your bedroom because you don't zing with any of them, perhaps you had better take this journey into colour a little more slowly.

How to bring in more colour to your Crone wardrobe

Begin with your favourite colour. A colour you just know makes you look and feel fantastic. Buy a scarf (and maybe some funky shoes too) and add it to anything you consider drab to liven the journey. That feels good doesn't it? .

I see your inner Crone light shining brightly. I see it glowing from the inside out, so when you wear colours you don't feel you zing in, well that is the overlay of what is shining to your world.

On the other hand, if you feel fantastic wearing something, you are vibrating with that energy and that is the fabulous overlay that shines with your inner light.

The following three poems are for the joy of the Rainbow Crone Woman that you are in your every-day life, rather than just for special occasions. Go forth and be a vibrant rainbow in all manner of colour. You deserve to be seen!

∾ COLOUR YOUR WORLD ∾

Colour your world with rainbows
And experience joy
Beyond your wildest dreams.
Rainbows are your soul experience
They are your reason for living;
Your reason for loving.
Acknowledge the rainbow within you
Say hello to the rainbow around you.
Feel peace in your soul
Feel love in your heart.
We *are* living rainbows
And we *are* the perfection of rainbows
    complete.

∾ COLOUR MY WORLD ∾

Colour my world red,
Colour it orange.
Make it Yellow or Green,
Blue or Indigo.
Let's colour it Purple.

No!
Make it all of these colours
And let's call it a rainbow!

∽ TOUCH A RAINBOW ∽

When you touch a rainbow
You put your hand upon your heart.
Each and every colour
Resonates with the loving person within.
Each and every colour
Determines our path in life.
So touch a rainbow today
And allow the journey to begin;
Not at the beginning
But as a continuation of the path you have
    followed
For an eternity.

Honouring the Last Bleed and The Holding of the Wise Blood

WHEN WE BLEED for the last time, it is important to honour what has been throughout our life, what is now and what is still to come. For me, my last bleed was in sacred ceremony with the Elders in Central Australia. It wasn't planned that way however it turned into a healing journey and an honouring of the journey into my Crone years.

For some it is a painful and confusing journey and for others it is a breeze. However, when your time of holding the wise blood arrives there is a need to honour the journey.

This is a time to nourish yourself in body, mind and soul. It has been quite a journey to get here; to this sacred time. A journey full of stories that have shaped you and tested you along the way.

Therefore, this time of the last bleed needs to be honoured and you thought I was going to write a sacred ceremony here, didn't you? There *is* a Gateway to the Crone ceremony in Part Four but I thought a more nurturing experience to honour this sacred time in your life was called for here. Call it a necessary precursor to ceremony!

This time, this very sacred time of being the holder of the wise blood, is a time of nurturance. This is a time to book a session at a day spa and one with the works!

Nourishing your body with a special scrub followed by massage, perhaps a hot stone massage as the rocks would love to nurture your body.

When you have nourished your body, take yourself out for lunch and have some soul-nourishing food and perhaps a glass of your favourite drink or a cup of your favourite tea.

Your body, mind and soul feel appreciated by the tender loving care you have gifted yourself. Go on, smile now at life. It's a whole new world out there for the Crone, the sacred wise blood.

Sacred Cauldron of the Wise Blood

THIS INCANTATION AND journey is a guide to feeling the power of your own sacred cauldron... the vessel containing your wise blood as you navigate your Crone years beyond menopause. This is a personal journey, not one to be undertaken in a group.

Find your safe place, a place sacred to you at a time where you will not be disturbed. Choose to work with the energies of wherever feels comfortable and safe for you. Work with this journey on the dark of the moon, the time of the wise bloods.

The wise bloods are the women who now retain their blood within them. They have reached the final cycle of life and this cycle is the most powerful.

This journeying will fill you up with the power of the Crone when you are feeling depleted by life's journey.

You will need

❖ Smudge or gum leaves and a feather to fan the smoke.

❖ A fireproof container.

❖ Matches or lighter.

❖ Deep red candle or black if you cannot find red.

❖ Pretty bowl or woven basket to represent your sacred womb.

Place your candle in a safe receptacle where it pleases you most to see it, such as an altar or other sacred place to you. Light your candle. This deep red coloured candle and its flickering flame represents the wise blood held within you and that you always have a light in the darkness to guide your way.

Place your bowl or basket in front of the candle. This represents your womb where you hold your wise blood close to you now. The journey has now begun.

Working with your white sage or gum leaves, place them in the fireproof receptacle and light. Blowing gently on the flames, you require only the sacred smoke.

Once your smudge is smoking, take your feather and gently move around your space, directing smoke to every part of this sacred place. You are cleansing your space of old stale and negative energies in order to create a light-filled inviting space into this power-filled journey.

You might like to say a prayer such as, 'Sacred smoke, carry away anything negative from my space and being.' Or you may choose to write and say your own sacred cleansing prayer.

Now direct the smoke around you, starting at your feet and moving up and around your body and back down to your feet once more. Place your receptacle alongside your candle, allowing it to continue to smoke as long as required.

Sit comfortably facing your candle and sacred bowl.

Take three deep breaths in through your nose and release them with a sigh. Focus on your breath, allowing it to become slow and steady. As you breathe in, you breathe in positive, healing and relaxing energy. On every out-breath, you breathe out anything unwanted and unneeded at this time.

Speak the following incantation three times. The first time will touch you in your mind, the second time you will begin to feel it deep within you and the third time it will settle into your mind, heart, body and soul. Speak out loud in a sing-song way as you read.

⌒ INCANTATION ⌒

Speak of the sacred cauldron…

For change is now so near…

Look into your reflection…
A healer held so dear…
The time and place is now…
To stir the pot of life…
When wisdom comes to visit…
Release all painful strife…
The healer deep within…
Will show the mighty way…
To keep the home fires burning…
When there's nothing more to say…
The time of change will come…
When you sacrifice all that is lost…
Remember the world begun now…
Comes with only love's pure cost…
It is only when you remember…
The world is fresh and new…
That the healer deep within you…
Is always ready and true…
Speak of the sacred cauldron…
A tool for the ancient Crone…
To journey to the realms of spirit…
For reasons yet to be known…
Her will is strong and courageous…
As she chants over sacred bones…
The time of the Crone is here now…
Casting those ancient stones…

There is always a sacred vow…
When one speaks the truth of the heart…
The sacred cauldron is waiting…
For you to seek out its path.

Sit quietly and close your eyes after the final speaking of the incantation. Place your hands upon your own womb, whether you have a physical one or not. Feel the energy of this incantation begin to weave its magic deep within you. You are feeling the power of the wise blood held now, the true power of the Crone. The power of this sacred journey flows outward to fill your bowl or basket.

When you feel ready, open your eyes and gaze at your candle and sacred bowl or basket. This candle and bowl represent your womb and the holding of the sacred blood. They are tangible reminders that you are a powerful Crone whose wisdom comes from the holding of her wise blood in her sacred cauldron, her womb, and it is ready to be shared.

This sacred journey can be undertaken anytime you feel the that your personal Crone power needs a lift.

Extinguish your candle and smudge and along with your bowl store them in a sacred manner to ensure you honour them, and therefore honour the sacredness of your own wise blood .

Invoking Your Crone Name

*I*LOVE THE SPOKEN word, it carries a great deal of power. There is none so powerful as a name. We have many different names in our life. The name we are born with, the shortened version of our name, a change in surname for many reasons including marriage, a need for a new name. Add a salutation and it changes the construct of a name.

In our Crone years I see that we need a powerful Crone name. One that is just for us, not for the everyday world. A name you can call on to remember who you are as a Crone. A name, that every time you call it out, will bring forward the beauty of this time as the Crone. I work with this in my Gateway to the Crone ceremony as a part of the journey, however, you may also choose to discover your Crone name now. A powerful name that is for you alone, as you walk the earth, as you gaze at the stars, as you weave your crone magic in your healing ways, and in your everyday life. The extraordinary in the ordinary!

Your Crone name will often choose you. Sometimes it is a name you have loved for many years and others will seek it in meditation. For me, I was writing instructions for my guests about receiving their Crone name prior to ceremony when my own just popped into my head. No effort required! Trust the name you are given. It might be otherworldly and regal, or it might be an everyday name. This name is a powerful reflection of the spirit of the Crone that lives within you.

If you are a Crone in the making or in your maiden and mother years, you can still choose your Crone name. The spirit of the Crone will come to you when you are looking for inner wisdom or to guide you to the Crone who will assist you on your journey. By having your Crone name available to you, you are honouring the Crone within you, even before you reach your crone years.

SEEKING YOUR CRONE NAME

On the dark of the moon, go to your quiet or sacred place. Light a deep red or black candle and sit quietly in the silence and invite the spirit of the Crone to be with you. You are entering into the cave of the Crone, the old one.

Take three deep breaths and release them with a sigh. Allow your breath to become slow and steady as you move into a state of relaxation and openness for the name you are seeking.

When you are ready, ask the Crone to share with you the Crone name by which the spirit of the Crone within you will be known.

You may receive it in that time, or it may arrive later when you least expect it. Trust when it comes to you. Research the meaning if possible and sit in meditation to discover what this name means to you, how it makes you feel and where you feel the name within you.

Whenever you feel you need the wisdom of your spirit of the Crone, or whenever you need to find an answer or just the power of her, call this name out loud. I like to stand outside in nature to do this. I say three times, I am (insert Crone name). The power of the name is palpable. Try it!

The Sacred Weaver

THE SACRED WEAVER is one who sees all of the beautiful threads of life and brings them together to weave a beautiful tapestry of experiences. Weaving the threads of life into a sacred tapestry is a powerful tool for the Crone.

In our Crone years we will pull together our memories, our stories, our healing ways, our wisdom and weave them into this next and last cycle of life's powerful journey.

In this weaving it's okay to have imperfections, the scars of life that are a part of the sacred journey. They make for an interesting tapestry. When you stand back and view it, you will see the whole fabulous tapestry up until now. There is space on this tapestry to add your Crone journey.

You are leaving a legacy for the generations to come, to know you and your journey.

Create this tapestry as a basket weaving, tapestry, painting or story writing. Your way of being the sacred weaver is the right one for you.

The following affirmation is to be spoken out loud three times to awaken the sacred weaver within you.

∾ SACRED THREADS ∾

I gather my threads
A sacred weaver of life.
The stories I share
And the threads I weave
Are the beauty of a life well lived
To the best of my ability.
I weave my threads,
I share my stories
With those who will understand
That my journey
Has been a sometimes bumpy road.
I have survived
I have thrived.
I *am* the Sacred Weaver
And these are *my* stories to share.

Come Sit at my Table Recipe

*T*HE OLD ONES, the Grandmothers long past, had pots of fabulous tea on their table and home-made goodies (a technical term for cake and chocolate). They welcomed and embraced anyone who came to their door with a story to tell, anyone who needed a listening ear and perhaps some sacred words of wisdom mixed in with the tea.

Women will come to know you as the story listener ready with tea and cake and know they have a true Crone sister to hear their stories. A Crone sister they can trust with their stories.

What you will need:

❖ Your teapot.
❖ Beautiful teacups and saucers and tea plates for your delicious tea cake.

❖ A candle.
❖ A vase of flowers on the table to set the soul-nourishing scene.

I am a great believer in setting the scene for something sacred to occur. I love the ritual of tea and cake and storytelling. The more you set this scene for yourself and those who come to your table, the more power is inherent within this ritual.

CINNAMON TEA CAKE RECIPE

Best eaten freshly made!
60g butter plus 15g extra
1 tsp vanilla essence
½ cup caster sugar plus 1 tbs extra
1 egg
1 cup self-raising flour
1/3 cup milk
½ tsp ground cinnamon

❖ Grease a deep 20 cm round cake pan, line the base with baking paper and also grease the paper.
❖ Preheat oven to 180°C or 160°C for fan-forced.
❖ Cream butter and vanilla essence with an electric mixer.

❖ Gradually add sugar and then your egg.

❖ Beat together until light and creamy.

❖ Stir in your sifted flour and milk and beat lightly until the mixture is smooth.

❖ Spread your mixture into your well-greased 20 cm cake tin and bake for approximately 20 minutes.

❖ Check your cake by inserting a clean knife to see if it comes out clean.

❖ When done, leave cake in the pan for 2 minutes, then turn onto wire rack.

❖ Brush with melted extra butter. Combine the extra caster sugar and cinnamon and sprinkle over your cake.

❖ May be served warm. I find it is also just as lovely fresh and cool with your cuppa.

Now serve your beautiful freshly baked cake with a delicious tea of your choosing in a lovely cup and saucer and matching cake plate. Perfect for a 'Come Sit at my Table' gathering and storytelling morning tea or to treat your beautiful Crone self.

PART THREE

All Crones are Created Different

*I*MAGINE... YOU ARE standing on the precipice, about to step into the metaphorical unknown that is the Crone. You stand looking at the beautiful vista ahead of you. A rich valley of opportunity and life. In the centre is a large standing circle of stones. Is this really something to look forward to, you wonder? Is this mine to own now?

You place your crown upon your head, feeling the power of this awakening symbol of the Crone, pulsating through your very being.

It's time, the Ancient Ones whisper. 'It's time to remember the journey of the Crone, her value in a world where you are needed'.

You stand and look, you listen, you feel and you are ready to have faith in your journey ahead in this last and fabulous cycle of life. The cycle of the Crone.

You have reached the pinnacle of your mountain in life. Your journey ahead is one of sharing your wisdom, your stories, your sight, your healing ways.

Take a step forward and walk down into the valley where those who seek you, who seek your wisdom and knowledge are waiting for you to share the magic of life's journey.

As Crones, we are all very different to each other and yet our journey into these wonderful years is also similar. We all have our own individual journey to navigate however it is with the support of the Crone network around the planet, that we encourage each other with our stories on this journey. We see ourselves reflected in other Crones and this encourages us to embrace this journey of Crone wonder. It encourages us to step up and be seen, to be vibrant, be sassy, wear the crown, dance with wild abandon (as the hips allow) and be true to self. Always being true to self.

I also see, in our uniqueness, that we resonate with certain directions in life, the cardinal directions and also with the stars. The following is my idea of who we are as Crones reflected in the cardinal directions and the central soul fire.

This is just the beginning of the journey of working with the spirit of the Crone and the directions.

Imagine a circle with the four cardinal directions and a central point for the Crone of the Stars. You may also choose to physically create a circle with rocks, shells or crystals.

Before reading each of the directions written here, step into the circle and begin to walk, in reality or with your imagination. Invite the spirit of the Crone to walk with you. Walk slowly, mindfully around the circle. Stopping here, there, here again.

One of the five points of the circle speaks to you. You are guided by the spirit of the Crone. She knows you well. She invites you to sit in this direction, close your eyes and feel it, deep within you.

Are you a Crone of the East, or a Crone of the West perhaps, or North or South? Perhaps you will look above as you are a Crone of the Stars. You will know. This is a time of trust. Trusting you, as you journey the circle, as you honour the Crone as your loving guide.

The following directions are guides only and as you accept your direction as part of your Crone passage, then you will build on the wisdom each time to sit with your chosen direction.

Walk your circle as often as needed and really feel the rightness of your choice before you confirm it with words. Walk it, to experience the power of your circle.

This journey may also be done when you need to work with a particular Crone direction for a sacred purpose. If you have a new project or need an answer to a question, then working with the direction you feel is right for you will offer some clarity for the journey. Call on the spirit of the Crone and walk your circle to feel its power and feel the pull of a particular direction. Trust your intuition. This is the direction for you, right now, for the purpose you have stated.

As the Crone, you are a blend of all of these energies and yet there will be a dominant one that you work with in the moment. As you grow through your Crone years, your purpose, your way will shift and change and grow as needed.

Sometimes, you will change daily and at other times, this direction is set for quite some time. This is a time to trust your intuition as you journey with the directions of life.

Following each directional wisdom is a meditation, written to take you on an inner journey through your chosen Crone Gateway. Sit quietly with the meditation and read the story. Take a few deep breaths and release with a sigh. Let yourself journey to that sacred inner place where all things are possible.

In each meditation you will walk through the Crone Gateway to the inner realms of possibility to awaken the spirit of the Crone within. Journey well.

Note: The directions reflect the Southern Hemisphere. For those beautiful Crones in the Northern Hemisphere, reverse North and South to reflect summer and winter and the energies within those directions.

Crone of the East – Air – Spring

CRONE OF THE East is full of grace and wonder. She excels at that to which she sets her mind. A mind that is full of joy and a heart that is full of hope. Crone of the East takes her ideas and dreams and offers them to the greater world. She is free-spirited and no longer allows herself to be tethered. Imagine a wild brumby galloping across the plains and through the mountains. This is the Crone of the East. As a Crone, she still harbours deep beautiful dreams. She is a visionary and works with the speed of the wind. She is a creative spirit, full of ideas and inspirations. She is a shapeshifter, sometimes still deciding what she wants to be when she grows up. She changes and adapts to new situations with grace.

Negative traits ~ The East woman can feel as though the world is against her when her ideas stall. She can also move too fast and miss the proverbial wood for the trees.

The East Gate – Meditation

*Y*OUR STEP IS light. Your innocence, your sense of wonder is the key to unlocking the East Gate. The Crone of the East walks through the East Gate, full of hope and joy for the newness of life.

Beyond the East Gate is a garden of colourful and fragrant flowers and trees. Bees and birds fly around this garden of love. You tread lightly upon the path that leads you, the Crone of the East, through this garden of colour and light. A warm breeze caresses your cheek. A breeze that feels like fingers of light, of love.

You meander through the garden and see a beautiful carved wooden seat at the end of the path. In the middle of the seat is the Crone of the East with a beautifully wrapped gift on her lap. She is waiting for you. You know the gift is for you. It is swathed in pink with a ribbon of pure gold wrapped elegantly around its edges.

You approach this Crone of the East and you see that the ribbon begins to fall to the ground. The closer you get to her, the more the gift becomes visible. The pink wrapping dissolves as you stand in front of her. In her hands is a beautiful crystal, a crystal not of this earth. A crystal that will sit comfortably within your energetic womb, igniting the creative Crone spirit within.

Crone of the East stands and offers you her seat. You sit, like the sovereign you are as she honours you and bows as a sign of her deep respect for you. The East Gate is yours now. This beautiful garden, this seat, this throne is a part of you now. You close your eyes and gently thank the Crone of the East for her honouring and her gift to you. When you open your eyes, you are once more standing at the entrance to the East Gate. You smile to yourself, a secret smile of inner knowing. You turn and walk towards your everyday life with a new sense of purpose, a creative purpose. *You* are now, a Crone of the East.

Crone of the West – Water – Autumn

CRONE OF THE West is the seer. She is a beautiful gift of fluid movement in her everyday world. Her ebbs and flows of life keep her interesting and interested in the journey.

She cries sacred tears to cleanse away the stories of the past. She cries sacred tears for the world because she is loving and compassionate to all living things.

The Crone of the West loves to immerse herself in water to wash away the pain of suffering. The ocean waves reflect her many moods, sometimes her energy is wild like the waves and sometimes there is a gentle calm.

The Crone of the West holds the mysteries of life and will share them only when they are needed. She is a healer, a seer of life and so often, she sees life beyond life.

Her wisdom often comes through her immersion in water, even everyday water such as washing dishes or showering. She loves to sit with her toes in the ocean or the river or sit beside a waterfall hearing the messages coming from the elementals of water.

Her intuition is strong, and the Crone of the West will never waver from what she knows to be true.

Her dreams are detailed and profound, symbols of the way of the world. She imagines how life might be and sets about creating what she sees and knows, even when no-one else can see what she sees.

Trust is a big asset to the journey of the Crone of the West.

Negative traits ~ The Crone of the West can feel overwhelmed by emotion when the pain and suffering of those she loves becomes too difficult to bear.

The West Gate – Meditation

HE SOUND OF water, dropping rapidly into a clear crystal pond below ignites your curiosity. A waterfall beckons you, a Gateway to another world that lies beyond the veil of the falling water and into the cave beyond. This is the West Gate.

You climb over the smooth river rocks to reach behind the waterfall and step through the cave entrance, the Gateway to the cave within. Walking forward you see that the walls of the cave are lined with flaming torches. As you move forward, the sounds of the waterfall behind you are left behind and silence prevails. Your soft footfalls make no sound on the floor of the cave. You keep walking, down and down, knowing that something awaits you.

Ahead you can see the flickering of flames creating light and shadows on the walls of a large inner cavern.

You reach the cavern and stop for a moment. The roof and walls of the cavern flicker with thousands of tiny lights. There is a lake that is shimmering with their reflection. A ring of torches surrounds the perimeter of this inner lake and beside it are two ornate golden chairs. A beautiful older woman is sitting in one of them.

The Crone of the West invites you to come to her and take a seat. She takes your hands and looks deeply into your eyes. You see yourself reflected within the deep pools of her eyes.

She tells you that you are a seer, with the ability to see beyond the ordinary into the extraordinary. She tells you that you are a healer, able to encourage others to heal the wounds of their soul.

The Crone of the West invites you to return to this space often to recharge your energy when you are working in these sacred ways. The waters of this inner lake hold regenerative energy for you so that you may do the work you came to this earth to do. She invites you to sit awhile in this quiet space and feel the nourishing energies of the cave which is symbolic of the holder of the wise blood.

After a few moments, you open your eyes and smile at the Crone of the West, who smiles back at you. You stand and walk back up to the entrance to the cave and the sounds of the waterfall. As you walk back through the West Gate, you bring with you a sense of peace and knowing for your journey now.

You are journeying back into your present time and space. Close your eyes once more. Take three deep breaths, stretch your body and return to your everyday world with renewed energy for the journey ahead. When you are ready open your eyes to your beautiful everyday world.

Crone of the South – Earth – Winter

*C*RONE OF THE South is the Earth Mother. She is the wise woman. She walks this earth anchoring the energies of the earth so that they may be made manifest in life.

She keeps her wisdom close. Her eyes show the depths of what lies deep within the Goddess and spirit of the Crone energy.

The Crone of the South is often grounded, however in times of stress she must remember to walk barefoot on the earth to release any stressful built-up energy within her. Her way is to teach others how to discard this energy.

Her home is her sanctuary. A place to regroup and ground herself. Abundance is a key ingredient to the journey of the Crone of the South. Her ability to create what she needs is strong with the heart of this Crone.

She is kind, forthright and wise, showing others how to get the best out of their life by putting down deep roots in fertile ground.

The Crone of the South knows innately when to be steady and firm and stay close to home and when it is time to take her earthy nurturing ways out into a wider community.

Negative traits ~ The Crone of the South has a need to feel secure and may on occasion overthink what she needs to do and procrastinate.

The South Gate –
Meditation

HE SNOW IS deep and pristine in its stark
beauty. You wrap your cloak around you, pulling
the hood down over your head. It keeps you warm as you
walk deep into the forest. You follow a deer trail, fresh
tracks in the snow indicating she is only a little way ahead
of you.

The going is hard because of the deep snow, but you
feel a pull to keep walking, keep following.

A light shining upon the snow draws you even closer.
You stop a moment. A clearing opens up in the centre
of the forest. A doe is standing watching you. You are
aware of the tall trees on either side of you as you stand
at the edge of this clearing.

The weight of the snow hanging in the canopy of the
two trees creates an arch, a Gateway through which to
walk. The doe is standing still, watching, waiting. The

only sounds you hear are your beating heart and your breath. Stillness, quiet, in every other part of this scene evokes a sense of peace.

You quietly watch the doe. Your breath is slow and steady now. You are mesmerised by this scene and your awareness begins to shift. The Gateway created by the overhanging snow-laden trees changes to an ornate golden Gateway. The doe in the centre of the clearing continues to hold your gaze as she shapeshifts and becomes a woman, the Crone of the South. She is beautiful and regal in a beautiful deep violet cloak, her flowing white hair adorned with a crystal crown.

She smiles and calls to you softly, calling your name. She invites you to walk through the South Gate and into the clearing to meet her.

You walk serenely through the Gate towards the Crone of the South. *You* are a Crone of the South. This is your sacred place.

You approach her and she bows deeply to you, honouring your right to be in this sacred space. Beneath her cloak she holds a crystal crown, mirroring the one on her own head. You bow your head towards her. Crone of the South does not speak. She places the crown upon your head.

You stand tall once more, feeling the power of wisdom emanating through your own crown, that has been activated through the crystal crown. Crone of the South bows to you once more and you know your presence here has been honoured in the quiet of this space and time. Offer loving gratitude for this sacred journey. It is time to return with your crown to your everyday world.

Walk back through the Gateway. You turn for one last look at this place. Crone of the South is again the doe. The golden South Gate is once more a snowy arch in the trees.

The doe runs towards you and past you, leading the way back to your world, the world where you, as a Crone of the South, will make a difference. Moving back through the trees and following the doe, you become aware of your everyday world, body and present time and space. Take a deep breath, stretch your body and open your eyes.

Crone of the North – Fire – Summer

CRONE OF THE North is full of life and passion. She holds a radiant energy that shines out like a beacon of light. She is inspired by what she sees and she is inspiring to those her seek to bask in her vibrancy.

She is a visionary who sees beyond the everyday. She sees the scope of what is possible and will go for the prize. She often has the backing of others in her passionate endeavours.

She is radiant in her beauty as it shines from within. She is colourful in her manner and style.

Crone of the North loves to play and show others how to play. There is something primal about the Crone of the North. She feels powerful, full of life and love. Her sensual nature is there for all to see.

Her creative spirit will birth many new artistic projects. Perhaps writing, art, gardening, cooking, or something totally outrageous. They will be just as vibrant as the energy she is feeling as the Crone of the North.

Negative traits ~ Like all flames, their passion cannot remain unchecked or there is a chance this Crone will, on occasion, be out of control and burn out before she has even begun to shine brightly.

The North Gate – Meditation

*Y*OU FEEL THE warmth of the soul fire deep within you. Passion for your life is waiting to be embraced. Stepping mindfully upon the earth, you feel the call of the Crone through your feet, through walking barefoot on this great mother, this earth. Crone of the North's voice is felt, rather than heard, through vibrations relayed to you via the sacred light lines surrounding the earth.

A sense of purpose and urgency fills you and urges you forward. Your steps are light. You know your direction without the need to be told. Crone of the North is waiting.

The sun is high in the sky, warming you, creating a sense of courage and strength for your journey as the Crone of the North.

A Gateway of Fire is just ahead. Will it be too hot to walk through you wonder? Crone of the North is waiting and she says, 'hold my hand and we will walk through together'. Taking her hand, you walk through the North Gate to the rolling hills of the land beyond.

Crone of the North turns to you and places her hand upon your heart. She tells you that your passion for life dwells deep within the recesses of your heart. Your own journey as Crone of the North is one of inspiring others to journey well and with passion and light in their Crone years.

The sunlight and warmth will always be available to you in this most sacred of places. Your courage and strength and passion for life will see you succeed in ways you never thought possible in these Crone years.

Crone of the North takes you by the hand once more and invites you to visit often and explore the sacredness of this inner sacred place. You are invited to journey far in order to take inspiration and the creative spirit back into your everyday world. This journey today, is just the beginning.

She releases your hand and you turn to walk back through the Gateway of Fire without fear of being burned. You are safe in this inner realm.

Standing at the threshold of the fiery Gateway of the North, you turn to wave to Crone of the North. She blows you a kiss in return. Walk back now, into your everyday world, into present time in your own space, bringing with you the strength, courage and inspiration needed for the journey ahead.

Stretch your body, take a deep breath and open your eyes. You are ready to take those sacred gifts offered to you by the Crone of the North into your life.

Crone of the Stars – Spirit – All

CRONE OF THE Stars is always looking to the sky. She sees the beauty of the stars in the inky night. She loves the different phases of the moon. She is in awe of the majesty and vast expanse of sky and feels a pull towards 'home'.

She has the ability to pull all of the other directions together to create her world. Her wisdom lies beyond this world and at times will appear 'out there' to others around her.

Her goals are to bring to fruition the plan we all came here to do. Her journey is not one of being singular, but rather one of many, here to hold the space of love.

Whilst she may appear 'off with the fairies' at times to those who don't get her, she is really connecting with the places that will download information for the journey of love for the planet.

Crone of the Stars has the ability to pull ideas together. She can see the benefits of many ways. As long as what she sees, feels and knows are for the common good of the planet and humanity, she will support the ways that will create positive change in her lifetime and beyond.

Negative traits ~ This Crone could become ungrounded if she forgets to also look around her at this great earth.

The Star Gate – Meditation

$\mathcal{T}$HE NIGHT SKY draws you outside. The inky darkness shimmering with a billion stars offers a feeling of being home to your soul. You lay on the cool earth and look upward. A shooting star suddenly streaks across the sky bringing a childhood memory and a wish is made. Another and then another, and you realise that this is a shower of meteors creating a light show like no other.

Planets begin to shine a little brighter. You feel connected with the earth beneath you and the stars and planets above. You breathe in perfect balance, earth and stars. Your breath is slow and steady as you continue to gaze into the sky.

The stars appear to move and create a Gateway to the heavens above. You know this Gateway is for you. This is the Star Gate.

Crone of the Stars flies from beyond the Gate and reaches down to gather you to her. Together you fly through the patterns of stars throughout the Universe, dipping and weaving, playing, dancing.

The Gate is closer now and Crone of the Stars stops and turns to face you. In your heart you hear, "to journey through this Gate is an honour for you, as a Crone of the Stars. Your destiny is to be a light of love amongst the chaos called earth. Do you embrace this destiny?"

You say yes to this honour. Crone of the Stars takes you by the hand once more and you fly through the Star Gate. Beyond the Gate defies your logical earthly description. It is pure magic. A place to return to whenever you want to explore this different realm. You have the ability to see beyond the mundane. This place that is home just as earth is home. You are a woman of two fabulous realities.

Crone of the Stars holds you to her, honouring your bond as you journey your Crone years. She releases you to fly back to your everyday world. You return to your earthly body lying on the cool grass. You are returned to present time and space. Take a deep breath, stretch your body and open your eyes. You are ready to bring more love to this world.

PART FOUR

Ceremonies

Ceremonies are Key, Gateway
to the Crone, Embracing the
Goddess Within, Healing Trauma

*I*MAGINE... STANDING ON sacred ground, pre-
paring for ceremony with other women, waiting
for the sacred fire to be lit, for the power of the sacred
circle to build, for the intentions to be set.

You observe the tasks each woman present is under-
taking, you hear the chatter and laughter of women
gathered together for a sacred time. A time of anticipation. Time out of time as the external world ceases to
exist for the ceremony.

Everything slows. Your heartbeat, your breath. You
have become an observer. The earth beneath your bare
feet becomes your grounding point, anchoring you to
not only the earth, but also connecting you with all the
other women present.

A drum beats. You realise you are hearing the sound of your own heartbeat as it beats in time to the heart beat of Mother Earth.

Silence now. The women are quiet. Ceremony is about to begin. Opening prayers bring tears to your eyes. You are ready.

CEREMONY SETS A powerful intention for you to change something in your life for the better. When you participate in powerful ceremony, you focus your intention on a singular outcome. Change.

The intense energy experienced in ceremony has a way of shifting you out of your comfort zone. When you declare what you want to bring into your life and when you release your attachment to old stories, something powerful is set in motion.

You make heart-felt declarations without being distracted by your everyday life. This focus has declared to the Goddess, the spirit of the Crone and your guidance that you are indeed ready to create change and you mean business.

Working in ceremony is a powerful experience. Remember that *you* are powerful because *you* set the wheels in motion to transform something, to create a healed sacred inner space in which to sow new seeds of light for the next part of your journey.

I have included three ceremonies I have written here. The first one is Gateway to the Crone and can be adapted to work with on your own or to create sacred space for gathering and ceremony in a small group. The second ceremony is one to connect with the Goddess within you.

The third is to help as part of the journey to heal trauma. The loss of a family member or friend, or the loss of your lifestyle or health can all be traumatic. I wrote this ceremony many years ago and now it is time to share it to be a part of the healing journey. It works with the power to tell the story and the soul nurturance you provide as you listen with love.

As Crones, women have seen many traumas throughout their long lives. This ceremony is one small step to assisting someone you love in their healing journey through transforming times.

Ceremonies are Key

$\mathcal{I}$ SEE CEREMONY AS a powerful event that maintains your focus as you state your intention for something to change in your life. When we want to create something new in life, we can easily become distracted by everyday events or the chaos that can be life's little challenges.

When we declare what we are prepared to create in our life, sometimes that little inner saboteur comes along and tries to distract us from our intent. Over many years, I have had women tell me that friends and family have called to say they want to see them on the day of a planned ceremony and want them to ditch the ceremony in favour of their visit. Or they or someone close will be unwell for example. Sometimes old outworn stories will rise into their consciousness to be examined and released and that can be a difficult concept to cope with for some. Challenges come along to test our resolve about creating change, in a very focused way, so it is up to you to stand firm and say to your distractions, 'I've got this. Thank you for your concern. I don't need your negative input. Step away from the change, and no-one gets hurt.'

So often, the people around us don't want us to change. They are comfortable with the increasingly invisible Crone we are becoming as we age. Someone said to me that a daughter said to them, you don't need a man in your life. You have children and grandchildren to look after. Seriously, young people seem to think that aging people are beyond love and sex! Nothing could be further from the truth.

Ceremony is a powerful tool to release attachment to old stories *and* to set new intentions for change. You are declaring to the Goddess *and* therefore the spirit of the Crone , that you really mean business. The Goddess recognises you by your energy or soul signature and set about putting life changes in motion for you. She knows your soul contract and when you are ready to create change through ceremony, she helps it happen for you.

I have participated in quite a few Indigenous ceremonies over the years, but Indigenous ways are not my personal medicine. When one undertakes to work with any Indigenous culture, one should spend many years learning under an Elder.

Many synchronistic events conspired to take me to the desert to be in ceremony and I loved every minute. These ceremonies were a catalyst for connecting me with the red earth and understanding that ceremony is key to working with the earth and to creating change.

Here are two more stories about how I was drawn to be in the desert ceremonies and the synchronistic events that took me there.

My first journey to be in ceremony was only a couple of short months after my fiftieth birthday and the intense pain of betrayal. This was to be my initiation, my first real journeying, by myself, to connect with Mother Earth, the Goddess in the red desert and ceremony, as I entered into my Crone years. However, my conscious awareness of it didn't know that until many years later.

ERNABELLA

Two years prior to my fiftieth birthday I began to have visions and dreams about being in ceremony with the Elders in Central Australia. Even though I knew that was something I wanted to do, I had no idea how that was going to happen. I had never been to the desert and

I didn't know anyone who had participated in ceremonies in Central Australia.

Each time I would have a vision or dream about ceremony, I would say to myself that's great and then promptly put it aside. A month or so after my fiftieth birthday I was offered an opportunity to head into the city of Melbourne to hear a spiritual speaker. It was on a week night and I had to work the next day. I didn't like being on the roads at night and I certainly didn't like heading into the city from my country-ish home. However, as I had just been to the darkest depths and was slowly rising into my light once more, I agreed to go.

It was still daylight when I headed off to my friend's place to journey with her into the city. As I travelled the back roads of country Victoria in the early evening, mine was the only car on the road. I began to slow as I could see something coming along the road towards me and it wasn't another car. I peered through the windscreen and couldn't believe my eyes. A magnificent chestnut horse was proudly trotting up the centre of the road towards me. No rider, just the horse.

I love horses and know that their symbolism is about power and freedom. This is what this beautiful messenger meant to me. I needed to embrace the power and freedom of the horse and take notice because something very special was going to happen this night.

I arrived at my friend's home very excited about the night ahead. We headed to the city and took our seats at the venue and I waited to hear something that would transform my world. I listened to the speaker and was disappointed with what I was hearing. Is this why I came all this way? I asked myself. Surely this isn't the message the horse gave me on my way here.

The speaker eventually broke us up into small groups and we were not permitted to be with someone we already knew. As we sat in our small groups waiting for instruction, a woman on my left leant over to me and asked, 'Are you interested in aboriginal culture by any chance?' Well that took me aback a little.

'Um, yes I am.' I answered.

'I have a friend going to the desert for women's ceremonies in six weeks' time, would you like her number?' she asked.

'Um, yes please.' I muttered, absolutely gobsmacked that my visions and dreams were unfolding right before me.

The next day I called the organiser and sure enough there was space for me and all I had to do was get myself to Adelaide and onto the bus bound for Ernabella. It would also cost me a couple of thousand dollars with the airfare and ceremonies. Normally, I would have said, 'I can't go as I cannot afford it.' Money was very tight in our household. However, on the night I went into the city to listen to a speaker, to meet a woman who would offer me the information I needed to live a dream, I had a cheque in my handbag that I had picked up only that day, as I had sold my antique furniture at auction, for almost the exact amount I needed to get me to the desert.

I had been to the depths of relationship hell and now it was time to test whether I would indeed follow a dream or stay home and keep bandaiding the old wounds. That trip to the desert was the beginning of my true path in working with women and working with the earth, and the Goddess. It was a catalyst for change and I would never be the same again.

YULARA

The second time I was called to the desert ceremonies, we were to go to sacred ground at a place called Umutja. When we arrived one of the traditional owners had passed away and there was sorry business to be done. We ended up at the back of the resort at Uluru at a place called Yulara. One day, a friend and I decided to take a little walk and meditate.

We walked the red earth to a place we felt was just perfect and as we walked away from the track, we saw the monolith that is Uluru just in front of us. She was magnificent. We sat on the earth and each entered our own meditative space.

I saw inside the rock. A giant pink faceted crystal was floating inside the rock. Underneath the rock was a huge sacred fire. I won't mention the rest here, but it was a spectacular meditation that was deeply earth-centred and feminine in nature. I was humbled by the power of this meditation but promptly forgot about it in the ceremonies. Once I left the calm and beauty of Uluru, I was heading to busy Sydney for an event. Uluru was far from my mind in the busyness of mid-city how-ever I was invited to head down to a local spiritual shop and thought 'why not!'

As I entered the shop, right in front of me, all alone on a shelf in a cabinet was a pink faceted 'crystal', exactly like the one I saw in my meditation facing Uluru. To me it was a profound confirmation of the journey ahead and the deeply feminine nature of my work.

The desert has always felt like my spiritual home but I know now, that wherever I am, is home in my heart.

Gateway to the Crone
Gathering and Ceremony

*T*HIS CEREMONY IS a lighter version of the one I created and facilitate for women as a Gathering of Crones to 'Come Sit at my Table' followed by sacred ceremony as a rite of passage to embrace their Crone spirit.

I have included it in this Gateway to the Modern Crone book so that women all over the world may work with it as a foundation to encourage the women around them to empower themselves at this most sacred time of life.

The detailed instructions will offer you a platform with which to facilitate a Gateway to the Crone ceremony. My aim is for women to embrace the ritual and ceremony of rites of passage for those entering into their Crone years and for those who have been in this sacred space for many years and who now wish to honour the sacredness of this rite and embrace it for themselves.

Although this ritual and ceremony is written for a small group, it can also be adapted in its wording for just you if you prefer to do something private and loving for yourself.

Come sit at my virtual table beautiful Crones. This is a time to honour the Crone within.

What you will need:

❖ Teapot, teacups and saucers, beautiful teas, home-made cakes, candle and flowers for the table. Oh, and don't forget the lovely tea leaves.

❖ Sacred drum (optional).

❖ A special place to perform ceremony, such as a garden.

❖ Archway to act as the Gateway (optional) or perhaps create it with some beautiful planter pots, or stones or crystals or flowers to create an attractive Gateway.

❖ A crown – can be made from flowers, crystals, branches and leaves or whatever feels good for you. You can have one for each attendee or one special one for your Crone guests to wear as they say their Crone vows.

❖ An altar in a sacred place such as a garden or in nature. Place something that represents fire, earth, air, water. Such as a vase with water and flowers, a crystal wand, a candle, a feather. Decorate your altar or table in a beautiful way.

❖ Smudge, gum leaves or other cleansing herbs to place in your sacred fire.

❖ Small firepit set prior to ceremony.

❖ Matches or lighter.

❖ Letters of release.

❖ Something from nature to gift your guests from your Crone heart to theirs e.g. a stone, feather, shell, crystal or plant.

❖ The vows to guide your guests.

GATHERING INSTRUCTIONS

• A week before your gathering and ceremony ask your guests to begin to write a letter of release. Old stories or thoughts of unworthiness to which they want to release attachment.

• Ask your guests to choose a Crone name (see page 141).

• Ask your guests to bring a plate of delicious food to share for a celebratory lunch.

• Have some lovely tea leaves ready that fit the occasion for your teapot!

• The day before or the day of your gathering and ceremony (because the cake is freshest on the day), make your teacake (recipe on page 147) or other cake that you prefer.

- On the day of your gathering and ceremony, set your table in preparation for the arrival of your guests. Make it lovely and inviting with your teapot, cups and saucers, candles, flowers and cake (don't forget the cake!).

- Place the gifts from nature you have chosen on each place setting.

- Set your outdoor firepit in readiness for ceremony and place your matches or lighter nearby. Place your smudge leaves near the firepit.

- Set your beautiful Gateway with flowers or an archway

- Set your altar beyond the Gateway, past the firepit and place upon it a lovely vibrant cloth, and your sacred honouring tools for the elements. I also like to sprinkle rose petals on the ground for a beautiful effect.

- Place the crown you have chosen on your altar. If you wish you may also choose to have your guests make their own from flowers or branches.

- Place the vows you will be asking guests to recite on the altar. They will repeat their vows after you have spoken them.

- If you are working with a sacred drum, place it near the door where guests will enter the gathering. Once they have all arrived, I ask them to wait at the door and I like to drum my guests to the table. It is all part of the ritual for me of setting a beautiful soul-nourishing experience.

• Time required including five guests plus yourself as facilitator: approximately 4 hours.

THE GATHERING

As your guests arrive get them to put down their handbags, and food for sharing later. Invite them to stand at the entrance to where the initial gathering will take place.

Ask them to please be silent and drum them, with the heartbeat of Mother Earth, to the table and ask them to take their places.

The intention of this beautiful gathering and ceremony has now begun in a sacred way.

Your guests will love the table setting, their gift from nature, and the sacred ritual way of offering time for getting to know each other through story-weaving, tea and cake.

Pour the boiling water into the teapot and let it steep whilst you begin to talk.

Open the conversation by asking what drew these beautiful women to participate in this Gateway to the Crone Gathering and Ceremony.

Encourage them to open up about their stories if they wish. Let them know they are in a safe, non-judgemental setting. A gathering of Crones is supposed to be safe and a place for storytelling and love. A space for tears and a whole lot of laughter as well.

Ask them if they have chosen their Crone name or if the name has chosen them. Talk with them about how the name came to them, how it makes them feel and where they might feel it in their body. This is a time of sharing.

When tea and cake and story sharing is done, it's time to head outside for ceremony. Invite your guests to gather their letter of release and follow you outside to the firepit.

Take your drum with you.

THE CEREMONY

I like to have the Crones stand around the sacred fire-pit where I will be facilitating the first part of this ceremony.

This will be followed with a walk through the Gateway, over the rose petals to reach the altar you have set up. Place the drum near the altar or table.

Once everyone and everything is in place, it is time to light the sacred fire you have set previously.

Light the soul fire and begin the ceremony.

Take a few quiet moments to feel your connection to this sacred circle of Crone sisters and the spirit of the Crone. The power of your intention to release old ways is already beginning to build now that you have entered the sacred circle.

Take a deep breath, in through the nose, hold for a moment and release with a sigh. Take another deep breath, hold for a moment and release with a sigh.

Focus on your breath – letting your breath become slow and rhythmic. Take one more deep breath, hold and release with a sigh.

On each in-breath, breathe in positive, powerful and loving energy. On every out-breath release anything unwanted and unneeded that may hold you back from fully immersing yourself in the power of ceremony.

The breath helps you let go of the everyday world and really connects you with this ceremony.

Offer thanks to the spirit of the Crone for creating this space and time for us to come together for such a powerful and inspiring event.

We invoke loving protection for all involved in performing this ceremony.

WELCOME

Welcome (insert names here). *You have entered this Sacred Circle of the Crone to release your attachment to old stories that have been a part of your past in order to create a healed sacred inner space in which to embrace the spirit of the Crone.*

We are honouring your journey that has brought you to this point in your lives where you celebrate the Goddess that you already are and the Crone you are now embracing.

Today, this ceremony marks a turning point in the creation of a new chapter in your life story.

SMOKING CEREMONY

Add your smudge or herbs or leaves to the fire so that they are smoking.

We are releasing any energy trapped within us and our auric field that may hinder the power of this ceremony by sending it away in the smoke.

Stand next to the fire and draw the smoke to you.

Draw the smoke to your body, front and back and say, 'Sacred smoke carry away anything negative from my being.'

Then return to your place.

Each guest takes it in turn to do this smoking.

INVOCATION

Note: In the Northern Hemisphere swap North and South.

We now invoke the powerful energies that are with us as we perform this ceremony.

We honour and welcome all of the directions –
We welcome the Crone and the spirits of the East –
the direction of air and spring. The direction of
sunrise and moon rise, the waxing moon, of new
beginnings, of birth, or blossoming thoughts and
feelings, of trust and innocence, of communication
and awakening from a deep slumber.

We welcome the Crone and the spirits of the North
– the direction of fire and summer. The direction
of the full moon, of warmth and passion, of ideas, of
expansion and growth, of prosperity and adventure.

We welcome the Crone and the spirits of the
West – the direction of water and autumn. The
direction of the waning moon, of sunset and moonset,
of release, of divination, of harvest, emotion and
movement.

We welcome the Crone and the spirits of the South
– the direction of earth and winter. The direction of
the wise woman, the elder, of being grounded and

anchoring your energies to this great earth, a direction of deep introspection, of home and fertility as we turn full circle back to the East.

We honour the sacred fire and welcome the great within – a place of being home to self – of spirit, of the fire within that drives us. We honour and welcome the Crone of the Stars above.

We honour and welcome the Ancient Ones, the Ancestor spirits, the grandmothers, the elders, the Goddess, Mother Earth, the spirit of the Crone and our beautiful soul family and soul friends today.

We invite the power of the Crone to flow around us all and fill us with her love, her depth, her power and strength as she holds this sacred space for us.

We honour the cycles of life – birth, life, death and rebirth. We honour the daily cycles of life and the changing of seasons.

We honour our sacred circle and the power contained within it.

CONNECTING WITH THE ENERGY OF THE CIRCLE

Take a few quiet moments to feel your connection to the sacred circle, and each other as we stand powerfully in this ceremony and with the spirit of the Crone as she guides us to heal a lifetime of wounds. The power of your intention to heal your old stories is already beginning to build in this sacred circle even before you release.

You are here today because you made a choice, to embrace the spirit of your Crone.

Ceremony is a powerful experience in which to embrace her to you.

The Goddess, and the Crone recognise you all as their daughters and granddaughters and their equal, and encourage you to take the power of this new Crone cycle into your life and work with it to enhance your world.

The energy created here today is felt deep within the core of the Goddess, Mother Earth and the heart of the Crone.

LETTING GO

We will place our letters into the fire one by one. We will watch it burn completely before the next woman places her letter in the fire as we watch the fire and smoke take away our doubts and fears and insecurities, as we release them to be healed.

Once all of your guests have burned their release letters say the following:

Close your eyes and feel the power of this release fill you to overflowing. You have now created a sacred healed space within you and around you in which to welcome the Crone.

We will now enter the sacredness of our Crone space. The spirit of the Crone is waiting for us all. Her energy fills this special space as you declare vows to embrace this new Crone cycle, as you declare that you are willing to be respected and honoured in your sacredness as the Crone.

Stand on the earth (rain permitting) and I will call each woman to enter through the Gateway and walk down to the altar. I will drum each of you into this sacred space.

As each woman enters and says her vows, the other Crones bear witness.

VOWS

You are walking through the Gateway of the Crone. You are ready to accept your Crone name. You are willing to tell your stories, share your wisdom, be bold and vibrant. Let us now move into the vows.

Drum the woman about to say her Crone vows to you. Place the crown upon her head. This is the honour of being the Crone bestowed by the spirit of the Crone by your side.

Ask the crowned woman in front of you to repeat the following vows.

Repeat after me:

I (insert name) and my Crone name of (insert name) honour the sacredness of this time in my life.

I embrace the Crone and allow her into my life without reservation.

I welcome the seer in me and the beautiful creative woman I have worked so hard to become.

I am the story-weaver. I am the Matriarch. I am the wisdom keeper. I am the Healer.

I honour my deepening connection with Mother Earth, the Goddess and therefore the Crone.

I vow to honour and respect my journey as the Crone. I listen with my heart.

I share the harvest of my wisdom with those who seek me out.

I... AM... the Crone.

At the end of each Crone's vows, gently remove the crown from her head and ask her to take her place to bear witness for the next Crone to be drummed to her place. Repeat until all of the Crones have taken their Crone vows.

Congratulations to you all. You have vowed to embrace the Crone and your personal powerful Crone name. You have accepted the power of your Crone self and you are willing to move forward with all the respect you so deserve as the Crone. You are already a Goddess and now, you are also a Crone.

COMPLETION OF CEREMONY

Close your eyes.

We honour where we have been in ceremony this day. We have accepted the mantle of Crone. We release the energy of this powerful ceremony into the earth, to bring forward to us, the next steps on this Crone journey.

We honour the spirit of the Crone for being beside us throughout this ceremony. We honour the Goddess for holding, with loving intent, this sacred space for us today.

We honour those who have filled us today with their joy. We honour all of the Crones here today who have embraced this next cycle in their life story.

This ceremony has now come to a close, but the powerful energy created here remains long after you have returned to your homes.

As one ceremony ends another is just beginning. Let us gather together inside and share the beautiful food we have prepared in celebration of our journey together today.

CELEBRATORY LUNCH

Gather together once more at your table with all the food prepared by each of the Crones. Enjoy this celebration until it is time to return to their own homes with the joy of this rite of passage into their Crone years.

What a beautiful experience!

Personal Ceremony to Embrace the Goddess

*W*E ARE ALL Goddesses. A beautiful reflection of the Earth Mother, the ultimate Goddess in my eyes. In order to honour self and the journey we are navigating every moment of our lives, I feel it is important to honour the Goddess herself as she lives within us. We are deeply connected with her, even when not aware of her. This mini ceremony is for you, to honour your deep connection with her. It is a lovely one to do before you go about your day or before heading into your sleep at night.

The Goddess, Mother Earth knows you by your deep soul connection. Each time you sit with her in ceremony, she knows you, she recognises you, she knows your soul journey.

By setting your focus in ceremony to connect with her, she knows you are ready to take positive steps forward on your journey and she sets about assisting you.

What you will need:
- ❖ Twenty minutes of your time.
- ❖ A special and quiet place where you will not be disturbed.
- ❖ Ambient background music.
- ❖ A natural pillar candle, in a lovely safe receptacle.
- ❖ Matches or lighter.
- ❖ If you are outside in nature, perhaps replace the candle with a clear quartz crystal for clarity and energy amplification or rose quartz for unconditional love and allow the sounds of nature to be your ambient background music.
- ❖ The mini ceremony outlined below.

CEREMONY

Find a place that feels sacred to you and create a time where you will not be disturbed. You are closing the door, so to speak, on the outside world.

Create a beautiful space in which to be in ceremony. If you are inside, light your candle, dim the lights and play some ambient music. If you are outdoors in nature, find a special place and place your crystal on the earth in front of you.

Make yourself comfortable, either inside or sitting on the earth.

Close your eyes and take three deep breaths in and release each one with a sigh. Focus on your breath, allowing it to become slow and steady. Imagine your heartbeat beating in time with the rhythm of Mother Earth, the Goddess. She has been waiting for you to make this beautiful connection with her.

Invite the Goddess to be with you as you sit in this sacred space. Invite her to journey with you throughout your day or into your sleep. Ask her for her guidance, her love, *her* power to empower *you* on your journey.

Say out loud:

I honour you sacred Mother

I am you,

You are me,

We are one!

Feel your connection deepen with the Goddess, the Earth Mother as you sit in this sacred space. Honour her for being your guide as you navigate the day ahead, or dream into the night.

When you feel the energy of your surroundings recede, know that the Goddess is with you in your heart and you are ready to move into your day, or into your sleep.

Offer your love and gratitude to the Goddess and release the energy of your ceremony to connect with her back into the earth. You are deeply connected wherever you journey today.

Connect with the Goddess in this way often. Each time you want to connect with her, try and work in the same space. By working in this space, you create a power place for you both to become one for the journey ahead.

Ceremony for Healing Trauma

'I am grief and I will hold your hand and your heart. I will help you explore the depths of your feelings and raise you up once again into the light. Acknowledge me and work with me, and you will once again know joy.'
From Grief to Goddess first published 2014

*T*HIS CEREMONY IS a nurturing ceremony designed to be a part of the healing journey. It offers a sacred and safe space in which the person feeling the trauma can sit and be soul-nourished by you. It is just one small part of the journey but a beautiful gift to someone in need of healing time with you. Grief comes in many forms. Often it involves the death of an old way of doing something before a new way of entertaining change or transformation in your life begins.

Grief can be intense where it literally tears away the fabric of your old way of being. This can be the completion of a relationship in its many facets, or an old job or career no longer being viable, your current social network, family or communal support is not currently available to you, a house move, a change of schools, health issues, retirement, your financial security has changed and many more situations.

Traumatic transformation that heralds grief can involve wars, natural disasters, accidents, the death of a loved one or political agendas that often have a sudden impact on you and everyone around you. At times such as these you may feel that you had no choice in the changes thrust into your life.

Often the catalyst for change is felt within you long before it happens, as a gentle nudge or a distinct push that declares the time to transform something in your life is now. You may have been asking for change in your job, relationship, home, study, finances, health, a new business venture or something else.

In these times of transformation there is an opportunity to dig deep within you and see the light of your courage and strength about who you really are in your magnificence.

Transformation can open a door and welcome a new beginning. Held within the transforming energies of your life is hope for a brighter day, a better way; a new way of being.

Landscapes are transformed, both within you and your personal life as well as physical landscapes. Man alters landscapes and so too does Mother Earth. It can appear difficult to process your opportunities when you feel held in the grip of the transformational energies that are physically generated by another. Energies that bring grief.

This ceremony has been created from my love for you, a fellow traveller on this journey through life.

This is a personal ceremony that acknowledges the intensity of the feelings you may be experiencing right now. You will have an opportunity to open the door to release an old adversary, often called fear, to make space in your life for acceptance of new ways of living and embrace your new beginning.

In the depths of your healing or transformation are the keys to adapt to new circumstances that will be followed with insights and inspirations for moving onward and forward.

These keys will be different for everyone. You will find them held in safe keeping in the depths of your soul.

This is a time to grieve the old and begin to heal and embrace something new. Remember, that grief takes as long as it takes and no-one can tell another when they will heal. This ceremony is designed to be just one aspect that may assist the healing journey.

What you will need:
❖ Firepit.
❖ Sacred stones to create a circle.
❖ Matches or lighter, sticks and wood for your fire.
❖ Sacred smudge, cleansing herb or gum leaves.
❖ Sacred drum for beating the heartbeat of Mother Earth.
❖ Healing ceremony and copied prayers for your guest.

Create a sacred space in nature with a sacred firepit and a circle of stones or crystals. Make your circle big enough so that you can both sit comfortably either on the earth or on chairs.

Settle your guest near the firepit.

FIRE CEREMONY

By lighting the sacred fire you are shining a light on trauma. Light the fire, allowing your guest time to feel its warmth, warm them deeply. Do this in silence and allow them to sit in the beautiful space quietly. This is the beginning of nourishing them with ceremony.

As your fire takes hold, speak quietly and gently to your guest rather than in a loud booming voice.

Take a few quiet moments to feel your connection to the sacred circle and the Goddess, Mother Earth. The power of your intention to move toward healing your grief is already beginning to build now that you have entered the sacred circle.

Take a deep breath, in through the nose, hold for a moment and release with a sigh. Take another deep breath, hold for a moment and release with a sigh.

Focus on your breath – letting your breath become slow and rhythmic. Take one more deep breath, hold and release with a sigh.

On each in-breath, breathe in positive, powerful and loving energy. On every out-breath release anything unwanted and unneeded that may hold you back from fully immersing yourself in the power of ceremony.

The breath helps you let go of the everyday world and really connects you with this ceremony.

Pause for a moment and then quietly say:

We offer thanks to Mother Earth for creating this
space and time for us to come together for such a
powerful healing event.

We invoke loving protection for us in this ceremony.

INVOCATION

Honour the directions and the nurturing guidance that
you are inviting and welcoming into this beautiful cer-
emonial space.

We honour and welcome all of the directions –
North, South, East and West.

We honour and welcome the Ancestor spirits,
the grandmothers and grandfathers, the elders, the
Goddess, Mother Earth, and our beautiful soul family
and soul friends today.

We invite the power of the Goddess, Mother Earth
to flow around us all and fill us with her love, power
and strength.

We honour the cycles of life – birth, life, death
and rebirth.

We honour our sacred circle and the healing power
contained within it.

Take a few quiet moments to feel the wonderful
energies invoked for this ceremony.

As the fire builds, quietly sit together as you drum a rhythmic heartbeat for as long as you feel necessary.

Your guest will already be in a semi-meditative space with their grief.

When you finish drumming, place your smudge, herb or leaves onto the fire and allow the living smoke to permeate the circle with cleansing energy.

STORY LISTENING

Gently draw out the story behind the trauma. Be a story listener. Listen without judgement, without interruption and without interjecting your own stories. This is about allowing sacred space in which your guest can just talk and where they know they are safe.

RELEASE PRAYER

Add more smudge, herb or leaves to the fire and invite your guest to say the following prayer.

> *I recognise and honour my feelings of* (grief, anger frustration, isolation, shock, transformation or they can insert whatever they need to express).
> *I release my trauma to Mother Earth, the Goddess.*
> *I honour this healing journey.*

ACCEPTANCE

Prayer and acknowledgement of changing circumstances. A time to open your heart. Offer your guest the following prayer to speak out loud.

My personal circumstances are changing.
I accept that these circumstances are beyond
my scope of understanding and control. I reach
into the very depths of my being to welcome
courage and strength to help me now on this
new journey. I open my heart to feel my courage
and strength. I accept that they are my constant
companions right now.

PRAYER OF INTENT FOR HEALING THE HEART AND SOUL, MIND AND BODY.

Offer this prayer to your guest to speak out loud.

My healing journey begins now.
My heart, my body, my mind, my soul accepts the
power of healing and love into my life.
I welcome healing and love with open arms.
I embrace my healing journey.
It is integral to my ongoing wellbeing.
I breathe in new life.
I honour my new road.

I take each step, however small, as it comes.

I pause when I need to rest; I seek help when I cannot cope.

I navigate my life one day at a time and at times it is one moment at a time.

I accept help when it is offered with love.

My journey right now is to heal myself from within.

Quiet times; busy times; in my time.

As long as it takes.

Encourage your guest to quietly reflect to themselves on their first steps forward into a brave new world. Peace is the essential ingredient for acceptance of inevitable change.

Drum the heartbeat of Mother Earth quietly for a time you feel is right for them.

CLOSING CEREMONY

Allow your guest to speak this out loud.

Love's embrace wraps its warm arms around me now.
Love is my salvation as I draw strength from my
very existence. I turn my face and my heart towards
the loving light of new beginnings. I know not what
awaits me, but I do know that love will be my constant
companion in its many sacred forms as I place one step

in front of the other towards a light-filled future.
As I heal the gaping wounds created in grief, love
will be my guiding inspiration.

Note: If your guest is too overwhelmed by all of the prayers, choose just a couple of intentional prayers to speak and adjust the ceremony to just be in this space, drumming and listening to their story.

Invite your guest for a cup of something warm and nourishing and perhaps some home-made teacake. Allow them to be grounded once more through tea and cake before they journey to their own home once more.

Dear Crones,

Gateway to the Modern Crone is just the beginning of this fabulous journey. A starting point of working in an energetic and practical way to embrace the beautiful woman and Crone, that you are.

A workbook for all women working with the four aspects of being a woman; Maiden, Mother Goddess, Crone Mother and Elder Crone is coming soon. An intuitive workbook that will bring in the four cardinal directions and working to heal, explore, write, dream, create.

Enjoy the journey dear Crones, Crones in the making and those women who resonate with the her.

If the Goddess and the spirit of the Crone are whispering, 'It's time', come seek me out.

With love

Jude

Jude Downes is a story-weaver of metaphoric stories for the journey and healing. She is Clairvoyant Medium and an Intuitive Mentor with certificates in Psycho Spiritual Hypnotherapy, Colour Therapy and Reiki. Jude's healing words work with metaphors through the power of story to affect deep & lasting transformation. She is passionate about helping others on their life journey. Jude is a 'Healer with Words' as she encourages people to write a new chapter in their personal life story. Her intimate connection to The Goddess ~ the Earth Mother and the messages that come from nature weave a path in the unity between mind, body, soul and emotions to form the foundations of her business.

www.judedownes.com
www.facebook.com/gatewaytothewisewoman

Other titles by Jude Downes

From Grief to Goddess Book
From Grief to Goddess Healing cards

The Story of Woman
The Mountain

Made in the USA
Middletown, DE
09 September 2020

18883309R00139